SUSAN SARGENT'S
the comfort of color

inspire • transform • create

Susan Sargent

WITH TODD LYON

PHOTOGRAPHY BY ERIC ROTH

BULFINCH PRESS

New York • Boston

Copyright © 2004 by Susan Sargent Designs, Inc.

Bulfinch Press

Time Warner Book Group
1271 Avenue of the Americas, New York, NY 10020
Visit our Web site at www.bulfinchpress.com

First Edition
Second Printing, 2004

Library of Congress Cataloging-in-Publication Data

Sargent, Susan.
    Susan Sargent's the comfort of color/Susan Sargent; photographs by Eric Roth—1st ed.
        p. cm.
    Includes bibliographical references and index.
        ISBN 0-8212-2867-6
        1. Color in interior decoration. I. Title: Comfort of color. II. Title.
    NK2115.5.C6S27 2003
    747'.94—dc22

                                        2003020959

Design by Lynne Yeamans/Lync

PRINTED IN ITALY

TO THE NEXT GENERATION: MY COLORFUL SONS, MAX AND BEN COOPER, AND MY THREE BRIGHT NIECES: LAURA, JENNY, AND HONOR SARGENT

acknowledgments

Southern Vermont is a hive of creative and energetic people, without whom these transformations could not have taken place. John Lahey and John Lahey III, of Fine Paints of Europe, showed us the glories of really wonderful ingredients, mixing our signature colors in their luminous Dutch paint. Wendy Galbraith created inventive window treatments, and we benefited from the skills of wallpaper master Betty Jaquay and painter Sandy Clark. Barbara Van Vliet, Kristen Wilson, and Erin Christie kept the studio fires burning and put in extra time with paintbrushes and tape, and Charlie Macomber, as always, kept us organized and solvent.

Special thanks to Judy Lake for her lampshades, and potter Jane Davies for her tiles. And gratitude to other Vermonters for their help with the project: Judy Pascal Antiques, Laura's Interiors, Mettowee Mill Nursery, Village Florists, Dan Mosheim Furniture, and Kit Mosheim Garden Design.

Artists Max Cooper, Horst Rodies, Pam Marron, Suk Shuglie, and Liz Maher shared their work—the final touch for the newly painted walls.

My licensing partners all worked hard to help us pull together the furnishings, especially Andy Pacuk, Joel Crisp, Bob Kyle, Pam Hausman, and Mary Macarthur at Robert Allen fabrics and Nimi Natan at Bomar trims. Other licensees York Wallcoverings, Lexington Home Brands Furniture, Present Tense dinnerware, Mohawk Home, and Oriental Accent lamps and accessories also contributed.

Our good friends gave us props and support: Simon Pearce, David Petersen at Maine Cottage Furniture, Ron Briggs at Hue, Janna Ugone Lamps, Bill Alsasah at Samplex, Stray Dog accessories, Koko bedding, and Wild Apple Graphics.

I must note our tremendous appreciation for the good nature and enthusiasm of the "transformees," whose lives we grew into for a few exciting days or weeks: Ed and Barbara Morrow, Barbara and Ben Van Vliet, Stan and Stephanie Hynds, Karin and Andy Nicholson, Astrid Viglund, Heidi Guldbrandsen, Paul and Nancy Schwindt, Tiffany Beck and John Teaford, and the Hunt-Evanses.

Thanks also to Tom Peters, my always exhilarating muse; Tad Stirling, who taught me how to look at rooms; Jill Cohen and Kristen Schilo for sharing my mission; and Cathy Mosca for copyediting right before my due date. Lynne Yeamans brought her incredible talent to the book design and layout.

And, most of all, to the Fab Four who shared the day-to-day dialogue, met our challenges with good-humored competence, and added special visions all their own: Gary Gras, Denise McGinley, my co-writer Todd Lyon, and most of all visionary photographer Eric Roth. Everyone needs good friends to depend on!

contents

introduction

With spring green under her fingernails and splashes of Inca yellow on her apron, Stephanie ignores the streak of plum paint just below her hairline and gazes at her glowing walls. It's like a scene from *Pleasantville*, the charming 1998 film in which gray denizens of a monochromatic town are liberated—indeed, brought to life—by color.

Stephanie has just had a makeover. Not to her face, body, or wardrobe, but in her home. The room is radiating warmth, and so is she. Clearly, the colors that now surround her have awakened something special inside her. "It's better than I ever expected," she says with delight.

This moment, or something like it, repeated itself over and over as we worked our way through the home transformations you will find in this book. And there is nothing as satisfying to a color fanatic like me as spreading my enthusiasm around and seeing the genuine pleasure that my "color team" leaves in our wake.

I have been obsessed with color all my life. As an artist, textile designer, dyer, weaver, painter, and interior transformer, I am a color evangelist, dedicated to spreading a message of hue and shade throughout the land.

I started my obsession early. Before I'd graduated from high school, I was making and selling colorful batik clothing. A traditional art education followed, but I found my true schooling in Sweden, where I learned to dye wool and create one-of-a-kind tapestries. For years I lived the life of a solitary artist. Though I had a strong following for my work and was collected and exhibited, the process of creating major pieces was slow and painstaking. For my more immediate color gratification, I looked to energetic bursts of decoration in my own home.

I was married and the mother of two, and our family's discretionary income always seemed to be dedicated to things more important than art and decoration—repairs rather than remodeling, college savings rather than new furniture—and I was forced to feed my color fixation on the cheap.

Paint became my best and most flexible decorating friend. With a good color and a brush, you can gussy up an uninspiring bureau,

Our color sensibilities come first from nature, and then make their way through artists' interpretations to our daily lives. Training ourselves to keep our visual skills alert is no different from maintaining an exercise program.

"Paint became my best and most flexible decorating friend."

re-imagine a bedroom wall, or bring to life an old door. During my years in Sweden, I had observed and absorbed a hands-on approach to "home improvement" (the locals would never have called it that), which was part of the folk tradition in my rural neighborhood. Carving, hand weaving, painting…my Swedish friends had modest budgets, just as I did, but they made a lifework of embellishing and decorating every surface of their rustic homes.

Under the spell of the decorative arts, I started my own textile design company in 1995, and named it Handmade Art for Living. A later tagline was "Exuberant Goods for Exuberant Lives." Today, I stand on a soapbox called the Comfort of Color.

My mission: To share my conviction that color, in the form of vivid textiles, paints, and objects, is a surefire way to beat the blues, as well as combat the monotony, lack of originality, and sheer charmlessness of most modern generic interiors. My goal, through color, is to achieve simple, unassuming comfort to nurture us in our homes—which are, after all, the most pure expressions of our individuality.

Still, preaching is one thing—making it happen is another. It was obvious that *The Comfort of Color* would benefit from a show-and-tell approach. So I took my color message on the road, scheduling color makeovers for eight homes, each different in profile. They would be case studies in different degrees of color immersion, each completed over the course of a few intense days.

My crew and I would supply paint, window treatments, bedcovers, wallpaper, and slipcovers but would avoid any structural work, plumbing,

"My goal, through color, is to achieve simple, unassuming comfort to nurture us in our homes."

masonry, or tile. We wanted to work off of what was already in place, and not force anyone to remove his or her best or most treasured possessions from the Designers' Path. Most important, as opposed to those terrifying TV makeovers that happen behind people's backs, we would fully engage the homeowners in color decisions, respecting their preferences while encouraging their spirit of adventure.

picking the projects

We wanted the homes to be places that most of us could relate to. No trophy houses. No expensively decorated palaces. No gimmicky interiors dominated by esoteric collections (plastic purses, gum-ball machines, African violets). No incredible locations (360-degree ocean views, mountaintop vistas; in fact, we decided not to show exteriors at all), and no

"It's way more fun to paint colors other than white."

McMansions in which one large and chilling space flowed into another (which would require a different approach and a much larger budget). We wanted a significant range of styles: urban apartment to country cottage, historic house to kit house, starter home to traditional Cape.

The people needed one quality: enthusiasm. A little trepidation is natural when approaching a dramatic alteration to one's living space, but paralyzing doubts wouldn't jibe with our schedule. Homeowners had to be agreeable to the scope, bustle, and general inconvenience of the makeovers and photo shoots. In some cases, they had to move out for a few days. In almost all cases, they had to put up with complete strangers (us) piling their clothes and possessions on the floor while we painted. (On the plus side, all the makeovers were completed over four or five intense days of fun, frenzy, and fix-up, so the dislocation was brief.)

A close study of the shades of a favorite flower can be a way to edit our paint and fabric choices.

We gave our color victims fair warning that what they were about to receive was on a do-it-yourself skill level. The members of my work team—Gary, Denise, Kristen, and I—are all handy with a brush but would never be confused with professional painters. And although the homeowners weren't required to do any of the work, they were welcome to jump in and help—as most of them eagerly did, which was an unanticipated bonus for both sides. (We might not have had the same participation if we weren't on this particular mission—it's *way* more fun to paint colors other than white.)

Our final roster of makeover candidates reflects the broad appeal of colors across ages, personalities, and occupations. We wanted different backgrounds and different profiles for our cast of characters, and that's what we got: two families with small children, a retired and relocated professional couple, a thirty-something bachelor filmmaker and his fiancée, a retail store owner with a vintage apartment in Maine, a family with teenagers, a high-powered banker, and an older couple with literary and spiritual interests.

the process

Once our locations were set, we worked up a color story for each home environment. There are behavior theorists who use color chips to get personality clues, and we employed a variation of the same system to get the ball rolling.

If you ask people to name their favorite color, at least 60 percent of Americans will say blue. (And no one says white.) But

"Find that straight link between eye and heart."

if you sit someone down and surround him or her with yarns, colors, paint chips, and fabric swatches, it is amazing how readily he or she will find a color that draws him or her in. A little simple color therapy work—I being the color therapist—encouraged our homeowners to find that straight link between eye and heart.

The process was surprisingly easy. There were clues in every home—artwork, collectibles, favorite possessions, family relics—that were meaningful, and, as you'll see, provided inspiration for the color transformations. And almost everyone has favorite flowers he or she can look to for ideas. In short order, the homeowners had a surprisingly clear notion about what they wanted.

Once we'd established a color direction, we developed simple project boards displaying paint or wallpaper samples, bedding, and fabrics for each room, most of which were chosen from my own product lines or those of kindred spirits from "ColorLand."

the goal

"When I wake up in the morning, I want to be glad." That's how Barbara, one of our transformees, described her home makeover goal. I loved that thought, and I think it honestly reflects the simple things most of us want when we are home. We want to feel comfortable, we want to be energized, and we want to be content.

I interact with colors every day. Whether I'm painting textile designs, choosing yarn colors for a collection of rugs, or working on a home project for a client, my mind's eye remains fixed on color partnerings the way musicians are always hearing chords. Of course, not all color is created equal. There are novelty colors that are garish, plastic, and cartoonish. But the ones to seek out are the shades that are intense but not screaming, bright but not fluorescent, vivid but not restless.

You can spend a lifetime leaning about color, and there is always more to know. In my work and in my life, I always try to find that sweet spot where color can be its richest, most harmonious, and most engaging. This book grew out of a desire to show how color can enrich our lives when used in lavish, comforting doses, and to offer encouragement to be free-spirited, creative, and—most of all—unafraid. I hope it inspires you to explore your own tastes so that one day when you wake up in the morning and look around at what you have accomplished, you, too, will feel glad.

Freedom of expression extends to letting our impulses take over. Here, a closet door gets a freehand makeover.

CHAPTER 1

chromophobia vs. chromophilia,

OUR LOVE/HATE RELATIONSHIP WITH COLOR

chromophobia

Color has an impact that transcends language and culture. Just as a good band with a lively beat can cause us to tap our feet uncontrollably and the first taste of a fantastic meal can make us glow with pleasure, color affects us on a visceral level. It moves directly from the eye to the gut, with lightning speed. A colorful room can flood us with feeling, making us excited, cheerful, inspired, comforted—or panicked, stressed, inhibited, depressed. But color is never one size fits all. It has cultural and emotional associations that vary from country to country and from person to person.

A bold use of color links this traditional interior to a modern future. A lime door in a periwinkle wall, glimpsed in the next room, connects to the pattern of the dining-room rug.

IN THE BEGINNING, THERE WAS OCHRE

In almost every early civilization, color was an intergral part of daily life. Before written language, Neanderthal people decorated their caves and the bones of their dead with yellow, red, brown, and purple paints made from oxidized ochre. Neanderthals surely had better things to do than mix paint—hunting and foraging come to mind—but their colorful art represented a kind of sacred communication, a determined expression of the creative spirit.

Ancient Egyptians—commoners as well as royalty—surrounded themselves with color. One four-thousand-year-old model of a typical Egyptian home displays red and yellow walls, blue ceilings, and columns painted with stripes of white, blue, green, and orange. Early Romans loved strong colors, too. When Mount Vesuvius erupted in A.D. 79, it preserved under the debris multihued rooms dominated by a color we now call Pompeiian red. In the sixteenth century, the age of exploration, dyes were a precious commodity, considered as valuable as spices or silk. Through all the subsequent centuries, Western decorative arts rejoiced in achieving saturated colors in every medium, from tapestries to glass to porcelain to fabrics, and in every level of interior decoration.

Yet somewhere between those color-rich traditions and today's, Western culture—particularly in dress and interiors—stripped color from our lives. What combination of circumstances and influences drove it out? To understand how we got to this point—and to suggest how we can overcome it—one almost needs to look back at some of the influences that made white the Holy Grail of design.

Paint is your most affordable design ally, and today's choices are endless. Better-quality paints use better pigments, so you get a more interesting and complex result on the wall, particularly with bold colors.

ENTER CHROMOPHOBIA

Even in the so-called Dark Ages, stony interiors were brightened with vivid textiles and paints. Color for art and interiors did have its own "dark ages," however, which corresponded with the rise of the middle class in Europe. Some would argue that this drab era is the one still wielding its influence in our homes.

As Western culture evolved and "rational" thought gripped the empires of Europe and America, color began to be seen as crude, even potentially corrupting. Nineteenth-century tastes leaned toward somber paintings, with dark varnish toning down the pigments. In a society newly committed to rationality, moral and spiritual refinement, and intellectual gravitas, color—especially bright color—represented everything the new establishment feared most: frivolity, emotionalism, and lack of restraint. Bright colors belonged to children, women, and primitive (i.e., non-European) cultures. Worst of all, bright colors could be seen as furthering sensuality—a sin that offended church, state, business, and polite society. With social critics and cultural restraint leading the way, chromophobia, a fear and loathing of color, was born.

The art critics of the time also weighed in with portentous disdain. The typical attitude was expressed by French critic and color theorist Charles Blanc (no kidding), who in 1868 condemned "the taste for color," calling it "a permanent internal threat . . . which, if unleashed, would be the ruin of everything, the fall of culture."

Strong stuff, and the public seems to have passively accepted it, despite some voices in the wilderness. The British architects Newsom and Newsom in 1885 ironically called white walls "relics of barbarism." Neutral colors and subdued expression were now equated with good taste and self-control. Goethe observed that "people of refinement avoid vivid colors in their dress and the objects that are around them and seem inclined to banish them altogether from their presence."

After being highly valued for centuries, color became forbidden fruit, associated with loose reasoning, slack morals, and unrestrained living. In this extreme climate, reason, conformity, and moral rectitude ruled. Color, like emotion, was to be managed, controlled, and subdued—and all this extended to the decoration of the home. There, order and decorum were expected to support sound principles of morality. Color, except in well-behaved, approved doses, was not allowed.

Breaking loose from formulas can liberate us from overly traditional attitudes. Here, a hand-painted cupboard with a yellow scalloped top.

are you chromophobic?

MOST PHOBIAS INVOLVE AN UNNATURAL FEAR OF SOMETHING THAT "MIGHT HAPPEN" BUT IN FACT HASN'T HAPPENED YET. People who have a mortal fear of snakes, for example, have probably never been bitten by one.

In the case of chromophobia, the sufferer is afraid to take risks when choosing colors for walls, floors, furniture, etc. By playing it safe, he or she ensures that no color mistakes will be made.

Keeping an eye out for snakes (or for a threatening wall color) might make you feel you have things under control. But paranoia rules out getting to know—and love—the very things that frighten you most. And by allowing chromophobia to keep you in its grip, you are effectively excluded from the creative bliss of making mistakes on your way to new, joyful, and expressive interiors.

common symptoms of chromophobia: a quiz

You like color and admire it in other people's spaces. Yet you can't bring yourself to commit to anything more daring than off-whites, midrange neutrals, or pale pastels.

Ask yourself: What stops you from trying a saturated, lively, or vibrant color in your home? Check all that apply.

- ◆ **It might make the room look smaller.**
- ◆ **It might make the room seem darker.**
- ◆ **You're afraid it will overwhelm the space.**
- ◆ **You're afraid it will look garish, faddish, or childish.**
- ◆ **You're afraid others will think you're crazy.**
- ◆ **You could get tired of it.**
- ◆ **It might be too hard to find coordinating furniture and accessories.**
- ◆ **Your family would never go for it.**
- ◆ **You'd rather stick with colors that you're sure will work.**

If three or four of the above statements describe your color dilemma, you probably have a touch of chromophobia. If you've checked off five or more, you've got it bad. Reprogramming is in order, and the simplest remedy is to buy a small can of paint, take a deep breath, and give it a try. Like that imaginary snake, color mistakes don't bite.

"Find the creative joy of making mistakes."

Of course, there was resistance, including artists who shocked the establishment with rollicking color and liberated brushwork. But overall, the out-with-color campaign continued on its unrelenting march toward modernism. Order and dispassionate design was the rule of the day. In the 1920s, architects already advocated white walls, and the Dutch critic and painter Theo van Doesburg declared white to be the "color of the new age, the color of the perfectionist, of purity, and of certainty."

Perhaps the most influential voice was the Swiss architect Le Corbusier. He condemned color, as those art critics had a century earlier, as "suited to simple races, peasants, and savages." He rejected all forms of decoration, and his dream was to have all citizens cover their walls in white paint so that "there are no more dirty, dark corners. Everything is shown as it is. Then comes inner cleanness, for the course adopted leads to a refusal to allow anything which is not correct, authorized, intended, desired, thought-out."

Le Corbusier and his disciples adopted this strict brand of modernism and spread the gospel with remarkable success. We are all too

"We are all born with a basic, sensual instinct for strong color."

familiar with twentieth-century minimalist interiors: walls and ceilings as chillingly blank as copy paper, with color and personality rigidly excluded. So complete was this tyranny that, as Tom Wolfe describes in *From Bauhaus to Our House,* Americans in particular were intimidated (or duped, according to Wolfe) into accepting these new, pure principles of design, from public spaces to the workplace to hearth and home. We have yet to escape.

  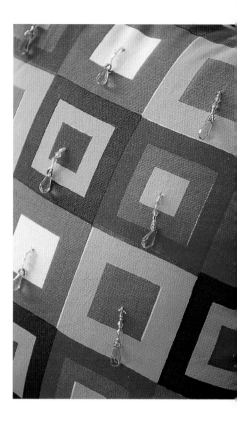

Chromophobia has a stranglehold that is particularly tragic in home decoration, the field above all others where we should be creating personal, colorful spaces to express our unique energy and creativity. White still outsells all other paint colors by a huge margin. Neutral interiors still dominate the pages of shelter magazines as examples of refined taste. Visit a major furniture store and beige or white upholstery is the number one seller.

The concept plays itself out in all sorts of decorating situations. Virtually every new condo has white walls and wall-to-wall carpeting in off-white that's completely impractical, offering a neutral background for an equally impractical off-white sofa. To a chromophobe, this must suggest the perfect, blank, unblemished life: no dust, unexpected guests, emotions, pets, children, or disorder of any kind. It says, if anyone is listening: Only high ideals enter here.

Beyond the West, white is equated with death. It is the opposite of color and thus symbolizes the pallor that occurs when blood stops flowing through the body. Chromophobes may assign to white properties of purity and refinement, but it is indeed a color without life.

chromophilia

If chromophobia is a snobbish distaste for colors, especially bright ones, chromophilia is the exact opposite—a love of colors, the more energetic the better.

A study done in the 1890s concluded that we are all born with a basic, sensual instinct for strong color, which is only later modified by culture. Children—to whom everything is new, and who themselves are new—have an insatiable appetite for color. Babies see color before they see shapes, and no matter how many colors are in the Crayola box, there are never enough. For most of us, the crayon box shrinks as we get

OPPOSITE: A variety of cool blues and greens sets the tone for this indoor sunroom. Painting by Pamela Marron.

ABOVE: Painting the inside of this cupboard offered another opportunity to introduce a new complementary color.

older. We learn to be conservative and to pass up colors that might rock the boat.

Dispiriting neutrals and white paint may dominate today's homes, but chromophilia has never disappeared. Confident designers have expressed their color-love in interiors such as Billy Baldwin's famous Chinese red living room for Diana Vreeland. For one brief decade, the sixties generation flung off the gray flannel/beige Formica lives of their postwar parents to rejoice in a wild palette. There are many distinctive public buildings that have kept colorful interiors—Claridge's in London has a tearoom with yellow and orange walls, and despite its name, the White House has its Red, Blue, and Green Rooms. There were other pockets of spirited resistance: Dorothy Parker's house in Pennsylvania, for example, was painted in nine shades of red: vermilion, crimson, pink, maroon, raspberry, russet, scarlet, rose, and magenta.

I believe that almost all of us thrive when surrounded by colors. I'm not just a chromophile, I'm a chromofiend. I love colors with a capital *C.* Colors that sing, dance, and dazzle. Colors that can't be ignored: mango, kiwi green, Prussian plum, fireball orange, Cajun red. Colors that raise your spirits and expand your senses. Colors that bring something to the party—in fact, create the party.

Colors have an undeniable emotional power, and science can measure it. A look at the work of Faber Birren, the world's leading color scientist in the 1950s, 1960s, and 1970s,

supports the importance of color in our lives. Birren spent his life examining the relationship between people and pigment, concluding that "any human being forced to work in an office or home surrounded by nothing but ivory or buff will hazard his good disposition and sanity. . . .

"Colors have an undeniable emotional power."

A circus is less likely to make a person neurotic than the tan waiting room of a railroad depot."

If we need other reassurance, we can turn back to nineteenth-century Europe and the British art critic John Ruskin. This eminent philosopher dismissed chromophobia and championed chromophilia: "The purest and most thoughtful minds are those which love color the most."

When we welcome people into our living rooms, the colors should be welcoming, too. Here, yellows, reds, and greens are echoed in the rug.

Ruskin may have been anticipating the joyous palettes of the impressionist painters. Or maybe he was channeling the spirit of Vincent van Gogh, whose color choices were fierce, in his dwellings as well as his paintings. In 1888 van Gogh wrote to his brother: "My house here is painted the yellow color of fresh butter on the outside with glaringly green shutters. . . . And over it there is the intensely blue sky. In this I can live and breathe, meditate, and paint."

Van Gogh was a fellow chromofiend who absolutely required brilliant color in his day-to-day life. It couldn't have been easy for him to stand by his choices—acid-green faces, yellow floors, swirling skies—as he constantly swam upstream against a tide of chromophobic public opinion.

Today's chromophiles must also swim upstream against the prevailing tide. It might be a stretch to compare our troubles or our talents to van Gogh's, but we too have to work hard to hold to our convictions. As shoppers, we are barraged by the conformity of goods. Finding well-designed and richly colored products can be frustrating, time-consuming, and often unduly expensive. An average store features two options: Safe Color (beige, burgundy, hunter green, navy) or Bright Color that is childhood garish (think Teletubbies, pink ponies, and neon rainbows). Products are so heavily circumscribed by retail dictators that we're left with the narrowest of options. Test-marketing ensures that no item should be "challenging" (i.e., interesting) or risky. We the people are presented with the lowest common denominator, stamped with the seal of commercial approval by stern chromophobes.

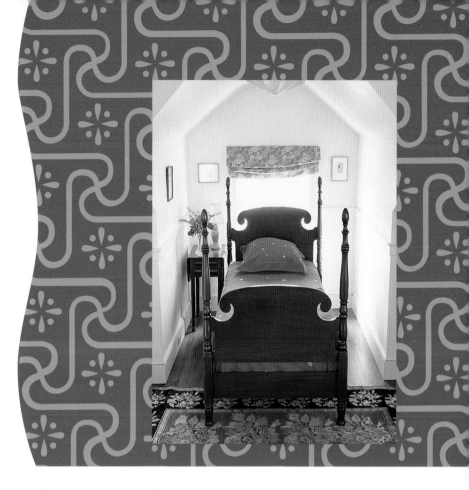

A four-poster twin bed is handsome in red.

Color is much more than an expression of style. It feeds our minds in a way that nothing else can. Norwegian color theorist Grete Smedal pleads that "colour should involve and engage people if it is to increase the quality of life." Opening our eyes to color—becoming chromophiles—changes the way we see,

"Colour should involve and engage people if it is to increase the quality of life."

—GRETE SMEDAL

heightens our awareness, and energizes our emotions. It enriches and enthralls us. As adults, our brains have the capacity to perceive an estimated 7 million different shades. Yet most of us forget, or fear, to use and develop this gift we are born with. Chromophiles unite—life is too short for beige.

light, color, and paint

MAKING A COLOR CHOICE IN PAINT CAN BE DAUNTING. Looking at a tiny chip under indifferent light, surrounded by more choices than we could look at seriously in a month, many people simply give up.

This may be one reason so many people choose white. Gloss white. Linen white. Antique white. Ceiling white. Parchment, aspirin, toothpaste white. White is safe, and there are more than two hundred shades of it in Benjamin Moore's paint collection alone.

There are also lots of excuses.

- **"White makes rooms look bigger,"** claims the homeowner.
- **"We can't sell your house if the walls aren't white,"** states the Realtor.
- **"Your lease doesn't allow you to paint the walls anything but white,"** says the landlord.
- **"It goes with everything."**
- **"It's restful."**
- **"It's not distracting."**

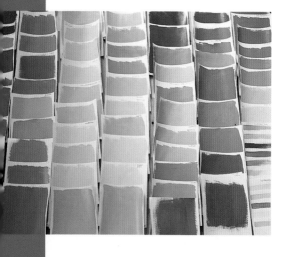

I believe white is chosen mainly by default. It is a decision driven by fear rather than by desire. Nine out of ten people poring over color chips in Lowe's paint department are too timid to allow their hearts to follow a color that excites them and too overwhelmed to trust themselves to make a decision. They're just trying to find a shade that isn't a mistake and doesn't make a fool of them or their walls.

One of the reasons it can be difficult to make color decisions, particularly for paint but also for fabrics, is that color doesn't stand still. Every minute of every hour, the colors in your home change according to the time of day and the lighting conditions. Geranium red window shades will glow like traffic lights during the day, then appear almost black at night. A favorite shade of lemon could look gorgeous under incandescent lights but hideous under fluorescents.

Personally, I never go to a paint store unarmed. Pictures from books and magazines are good, but even better are fabric swatches or something that you love from your home—a scarf, a plate, a pair of socks. (I once

went to a paint store in New York City with two cobalt mixing bowls under my arm and found exactly the match I was looking for.) Once there, select a group of paint chips that are close to your idea or that are good matches for whatever you brought with you and then leave—immediately. It is perilous to linger long enough to let your eye wander, as paralysis might set in. And who could make a decision for a whole room using a one-inch square of color under bad lighting, far from the mother ship?

Once back home, you can narrow down your choices to a couple you really like. I suggest testing a sample during different times of the day in your existing space. Not only will it look different, your mood and relationship to the color will change, too. It is also important to think through what times of day you use that room and what you want the color to do: encourage socializing, put you to sleep, soothe you, stimulate you, etc. Paint big pieces of poster board with a disposable sponge brush, and tack them up in the room you're thinking about. Some paint companies now

offer overscale paint chips up to 18 by 24 inches for about five dollars. Look at them in every light from dawn to midnight, move them around, let them sink in.

Remember: *It's only paint.* It's not marriage, it's not your firstborn, and your job and mortgage are not on the line. There are no color police out there deducting points in some heavenly account book if you make a mistake. Your house has its own location, natural light conditions, and functions. And you have your own associations, emotions, histories, and visual processes that will let you find the colors that are right—with or without an expert.

"The purest and most thoughtful minds are those which love color the most."

—JOHN RUSKIN

THIS PAGE: A stairwell is a good place for whimsy. My son Max and I collaborated on a painted wall (by me) and a row of paintings (by him.)
OPPOSITE, TOP: An old-fashioned washstand for a modern bathroom was devised using a vintage bureau and a classic bowl sink. Jane Davies made the leaf tiles.
OPPOSITE, BOTTOM: I love painted floors, and this old house has a variety of unexpected colors.

working notes

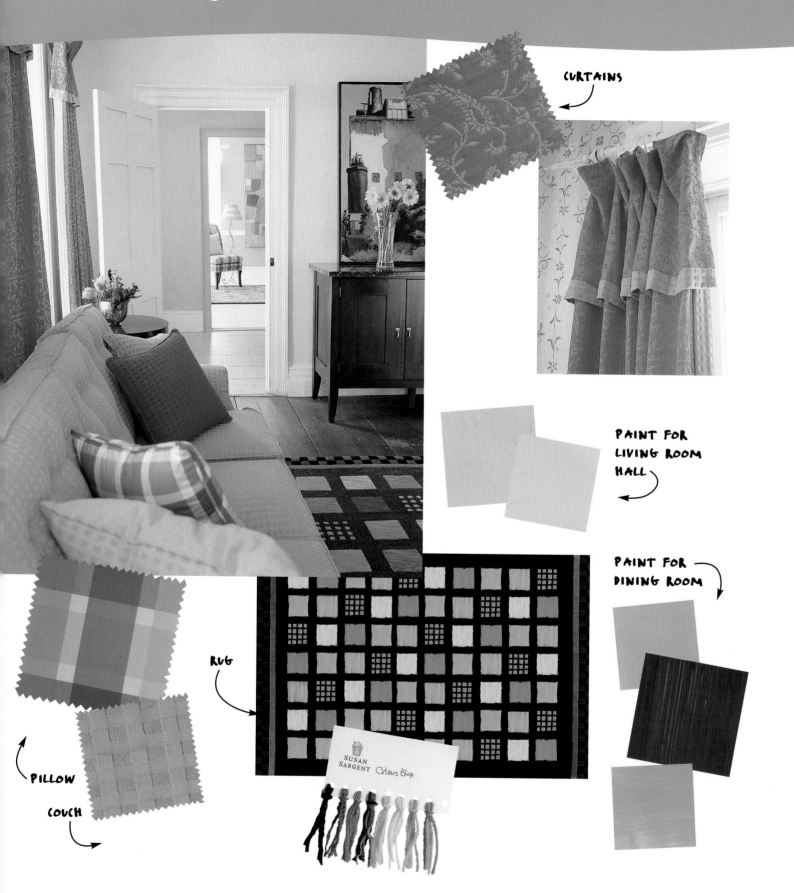

CURTAINS

PAINT FOR
LIVING ROOM
HALL

PAINT FOR
DINING ROOM

RUG

SUSAN
SARGENT Citrus Blox

PILLOW

COUCH

DUVET

Birds in a Bush

SUSAN SARGENT

RUG

PAINT FOR SUNROOM

PILLOWS

CHAIR

PAINT FOR UPSTAIRS HALL

PAINT FOR DOWNSTAIRS BEDROOM

CHAPTER 2

the tao of
decorating

Color is not a drug, in spite of what certain
ancient philosophers believed. Nor is height-
ened color awareness necessarily a by-product
of hallucinogens, no matter what acid-dropping
hippies from the 1960s wrote in their journals.

But color can elevate our mood and fill
our senses almost to the point of intoxication,
and it can indeed be addictive. I know from
personal experience that once you've gotten a
taste of it, you'll want more. Color experimen-
tation can definitely lead to color dependence.
Like pleasures such as jogging, gardening,
and reading, color is another addiction that
nobody wants to recover from.

Consider the case of Barbara and Ed
Morrow. They spent most of their lives as
chromo-apathetics who never thought much
about color one way or the other. Last year
they agreed to have their house made over
with vibrant paints and textiles. Though a bit
tentative at first—"I could never live with
this," said Barbara when she first walked
through an orange room—it was only a
matter of months before the two of them
became bona fide color fiends.

HARMONY ACHIEVED: The living room is painted
a perfect terra-cotta, a foil for the owner's apricot wing
chair, bronze Buddha, antique Guatemalan sideboard,
and Klee print.

"Color can elevate our mood and fill our senses."

The story goes like this: Barbara and Ed's lovely old home, built about 1860, has always been a model of gracious architecture. On the ground floor are spacious rooms with good flow, high ceilings, built-in cabinets, French doors, and oversize windows. On the second floor, at the top of a gently curving stairway, is the kind of generous landing that accommodates all the crisscrossings of a large family. At its perimeter are doors opening into three cozy bedrooms, and in its center is a linen cupboard with nicely detailed paneled doors, and a reading alcove in a sunny window.

ABOVE: A detail of the hand-stenciled screen, which was lightly sanded after painting for a stonewashed feel.

OPPOSITE: A screen can soften the corners of a large room. The painting was bought in Ecuador in the late sixties.

The house had everything going for it, except personality. With white walls and gray carpeting, the interior wasn't nearly as interesting as its residents. Barbara and Ed have lived in Guatemala, Ecuador, and Algeria and for the past twenty-six years have owned one of the most respected independent bookstores in the United States. The couple has also raised a family, collected art, provided a home away from home for numerous visiting authors, and served countless meals from Barbara's gourmet kitchen. They are both Buddhists and for years hosted a meditation group that met weekly in their living room. Understandably, the decoration of their home took a backseat to their busy lives. There was little opportunity to make changes, and nothing much was done to make it as exciting as it could be.

"It was drab," admitted Barbara of the living room. "For meetings, we'd push the furniture into the corners and pile cushions on the floor. The only colorful elements were the Tibetan prayer flags that hung in the window."

The flags—unabashed compositions in blue, yellow, and hot red—served as focal points during meditation sessions. Although I'm not a Buddhist, they also inspired me and helped direct Barbara and Ed's future palette.

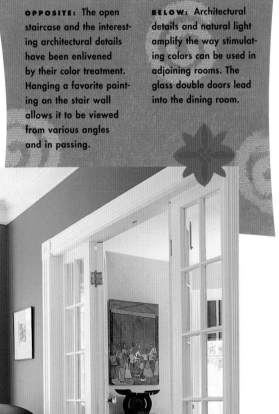

OPPOSITE: The open staircase and the interesting architectural details have been enlivened by their color treatment. Hanging a favorite painting on the stair wall allows it to be viewed from various angles and in passing.

BELOW: Architectural details and natural light amplify the way stimulating colors can be used in adjoining rooms. The glass double doors lead into the dining room.

OPPOSITE: Vintage furniture in the dining room went from ignored to shining in the light of the new golden walls. The wall color was selected based on the bright fabric used for the shades.

LEFT: The bold stripe is used again on the table runner and napkins.

BELOW: The corner china cupboard packs a punch with its new lime interior and goes from merely "storage" to a new design element.

OPPOSITE: This corner of the family room gets the most use, and its casual feel is just right for everyday moments.

ABOVE: A bookcase is the visual divider between the sitting and dining ends of the long room.

the path to color enlightenment

My mission was to guide a colorful couple to a colorful home. When I came on the scene, the living room was no longer used as a meditation mecca—the weekly group had gotten too big and had moved to another location. It was the perfect time to launch a makeover. Barbara and Ed had long planned to tear up the colorless carpeting and put down hardwood. Once the floors were done, we had wonderful rooms that were ready to be brought to life.

The living room was liberated first. Its transformation began with a modern, subdued floral paisley fabric that Barbara had chosen for the sofa. From this pattern we pulled a delicious earthy-red shade for the new wall paint.

INSPIRATION

A PLAY OF TEXTURES:
Flowers, pottery, a silk
runner, and a rustic wooden
sideboard resonate against
the bold wall.

ment so quiet that it disappeared from view.
Would they now shield their eyes and hide?
Would they avoid their passion-red parlor and
seek refuge in the bathtub or a corner of the
kitchen? Would they feel like color victims of
my mad obsession? Or worst of all, would
the new colors and patterns erase the spiritual
connection they'd once known there?

Thankfully, no. "Tibetan Buddhism is all
about awareness," explained Barbara. "Colors
are stimulating, which is why many Buddhist
shrine rooms are very bright. The idea is to be
awake, aware of your environment, observing
your mind."

Barbara and Ed were indeed awakened and
felt as if a new landscape had bloomed under
their roof. But their excitement was as much
social as spiritual. "Nobody wanted to be here
before," said Ed of the living room. "Even
when there were a lot of people over, we all
crowded into the kitchen. Now, it's a great
place for entertaining."

Barbara agreed: "The living room was
returned to us."

the wheel of life meets the color wheel

Room by room, the house came alive. The
adjacent dining room and sitting room were
painted graduated shades of saffron yellow
and were accessorized with fabrics and rugs
that introduced spicy accent colors: paprika,
curry, and wasabi.

Upstairs, the bedrooms were made over
with paints and fabrics that alternated between
dreamy blues and refreshing greens, enlivened
with an occasional splash of red.

Well before the project was finished,
Barbara and Ed had become full-blown color

As the red paint was being applied, I had
the strange sensation that the old white paint
was being scraped off the walls, revealing
the living room's true color beneath. It was
as if the space had always been red and had
been hiding behind a plain wrapper for years,
waiting to make its debut.

The change was dramatic. But I wondered:
Was it also traumatic? Barbara and Ed had
become accustomed to a stark, Zen-like environ-

CLOCKWISE, FROM LEFT: A gorgeous radiator has its own design zip. Mixed textures for handmade cotton and linen pillows. A colorful vase of flowers draws the eye in the green bedroom. A liberating dose of pattern in blues and reds.

ABOVE, TOP: Branches in a vase mimic the blue vine design on the bedroom chair.

ABOVE, BOTTOM: More blue clues on the landing, where a floral rug leads into the bedroom beyond. The orange bench is an accent note.

OPPOSITE: This blue bedroom incorporates soft florals in periwinkle shades. The built-in shelves are in four shades of blues and teals. By painting only the drawer fronts, the white trim is left to break up the clear blue wall behind.

OPPOSITE: The soft green of the walls make this master bedroom a welcome place for quiet thoughts. Touches of orange and red keep the senses awake and connect to the reading chair on the landing and staircase wall beyond.

ABOVE: The bed reflected in a closet mirror.
BELOW: A detail of the curtain tiebacks.

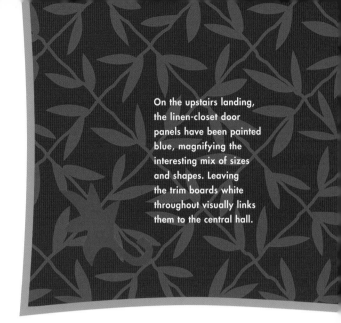

converts. "Right from the beginning, when we started looking at swatches, I started dreaming about color and haven't stopped," said Barbara. "The way I see color has changed; my consciousness has been raised to a whole new level of appreciation. It's quite extraordinary."

I got my first hint of Barbara's budding chromophilia in her kitchen. Though it was an important player in the home's open floor plan and directly overlooked the sitting room, I hadn't identified it as a priority for a color makeover. It was dominated by dark wood cabinets, with precious little wall space in which to make a difference.

But Barbara couldn't stand how dreary her kitchen looked in contrast to the lively rooms around it. She couldn't rest until we had picked another color to rejuvenate the shadowy space. A soft gray-green, linked to another fabric across the room, was put in. She was satisfied by the kitchen paint job, but not for long: "It's the one color in the house I'm not sure of," she says today. Why? "It's too subdued."

I knew Barbara and Ed had become hard-core chromophiles when they challenged the color of the wall that flanked the stairway to the second floor. The stairway rises up in one

showcasing artwork

FOR AS FAR BACK AS WE CAN REMEMBER, ART GALLERY WALLS HAVE BEEN PAINTED STARK WHITE. It's a given in the world of art display. Curators have long depended on white walls to disappear from viewers' conscious vision, leaving the focus entirely on the colors and shapes of the works on display. For years, white-cube galleries—those seamless, colorless, antiseptic spaces—have been the standard choice for art exhibitions.

"The way I see color has changed; my consciousness has been raised."
—BARBARA MORROW

And as the world became more democratic, access to art became broader and less rigid. The taillights of history shine kindly on those artists who were brave enough to create art for art's sake and who showed their work in plain white spaces that looked nothing like palaces or cathedrals.

Yet what is appropriate for galleries and palaces is less so for most of us in our normal homescapes. We all aspire to owning art, whatever our budget, and the good news is that anything goes: posters, photographs, trash-can lids—we are much less restricted about what we hang, and for most of us, if we like it, on the wall it goes.

While the definition of art for the home has broadened, the choices in wall color have not kept pace. It's still white, white, white. It's all part of the "chilly white interior" style of modern architecture that rules the landscape. The pictures might be colorful, but the walls must be white.

It's time for a change. After a lifetime of viewing art in white-cube galleries, I am in rebellion. Although I'm not interested in returning to the days of parlor-style exhibits, I refuse to believe that colorful walls aren't appropriate for displaying works of art.

Barbara and Ed can back me up. When I first observed their home, they had a number of book-related posters on their white walls, plus a few original

It wasn't always this way. Before "modern" sensibilities emerged in Europe, galleries looked like private parlors, with soaring walls painted in rich colors, articulated by crown molding, inset panels, and architectural flourishes. Those walls would be covered in framed paintings, hung left to right and top to bottom, from floor to ceiling.

One could argue that premodern galleries diminished works of art by presenting them as mere decorative objects—pricey status symbols for upper-class homes.

Prado has exhibition areas with sand pink walls, and the National Gallery in London has adopted colors to showcase the work of significant artists.

At home, art should be a part of our daily lives. We should hang out with it, ignore it, or revel in it as the mood strikes. Wall color doesn't have to fight with art—it can enhance it and make it glow. It doesn't require sterility to be acknowledged. A personal art collection is never static; it changes with time and taste, evolving right along with our relationships, our philosophies, and our color sense.

As the curator of your personal space, you have unlimited options. Whether you're hanging an important oil painting, flea market curiosities, vintage photographs, Great-Aunt Ethel's watercolors, your own sketches, or children's finger paintings, think about using an outspoken wall color to enhance your collection and make your favorite works of art seem more beautiful and special than ever.

artworks gathered during their travels or given to them by friends. As their home was being transformed with sizzling new colors, Ed and Barbara decided to raid the basement and unearth their forgotten art collection. In storage were a number of ethnic paintings and framed textiles they had collected years ago in South America, as well as a few nice prints Ed had inherited from his parents. Once exposed to the cayenne red living room and the curry yellow dining room, the pieces became gorgeous. "The artwork never looked like this before," said an awed Barbara. "I hadn't paid attention to this stuff for years; now it's taken on a whole new life."

Barbara and Ed are not alone. Galleries, studios, even major museums are finally rejecting the heavy history of the white wall and are presenting art in spaces painted orange, red, blue, green, brown, black— whatever makes the work most compelling. Spain's

For that stair wall, we'd picked another subtle, whispery green, to build a bridge between the spicy red living room and the cool blues and greens upstairs. I knew the low-key stairway would help with the transition. But to Barbara and Ed, whose eyes had been deprived of color for years, that stairway wall was downright boring. With all the fervor of the newly converted, they demanded more flash. They saw the bashful paint as deadweight, an underachieving color in a house full of high-key hues they'd come to delight in.

The story of the stairway ended well. There was a piece of Guatemalan art in Barbara and Ed's collection whose colors redeemed the quiet wall and tied the upstairs to the downstairs in a most satisfying way. But I wouldn't be surprised to go back one day and find a different color glowing in that staircase.

The wheel of life had definitely turned. At the beginning of the project, it was I who was pitching lively colors to Barbara and Ed; at the end, they were resisting neutrals and pitching lively colors to me.

corner of the living room, and that wall is visible and connected to the entire downstairs.

As much as I love jazzy colors, the eye needs places to rest. A bit of quiet here and there is healthy; it prevents colorful spaces from becoming overwhelming and, in quintessential yin/yang fashion, underscores their intensity. I find these quiet zones essential to building vivid colors in a livable home.

lost spaces, found again

LOOK AROUND YOUR HOME. DO YOU HAVE ANY OVERLOOKED SPACES, ANY FORGOTTEN LITTLE AREAS THAT ARE WAITING TO BE REVEALED BY PAINT? Peer inside closets, pantries, alcoves. Look behind the books on your shelves, at the inside of medicine cabinets, or at an isolated corner of your kitchen. Check out door panels and observe the architecture of foyers, landings, dormers, or any spot that's so familiar that you've ceased to notice it.

These nooks and crannies don't have to hide in the background. In fact, each offers an opportunity for expression. With nothing more than a quart of paint, you can call these spaces out, get them noticed, and make them add wit and whimsy to the four corners of your home.

There's something magical about opening a closet door and finding a surprising color inside—floor, ceiling, and walls. It says, Somebody took care of this little, neglected space and gave it some heart.

In a corner of Barbara and Ed's red living room is a doorway and beyond that a little window on a mysterious wall painted spring green. (Okay, it's a coat closet and an entryway to the powder room, but it's still mysterious.) That green has all the magic of a peek around the door on Christmas morning and turns the corner from invisible to shimmering. A nice old china cabinet in their dining room is revved up with the same shade of green, applied to its interior. Plates and dinnerware now nestle in a glowing bed of color, and the entire cupboard got an updated glory. Upstairs, built-in drawers that were once invisible gain attention by blue-painted panels that highlight their design.

These are small things, which take little time and are surprisingly gratifying. Not everyone is ready to go wild on their walls. But little spaces can be the perfect way to experiment with colors, add a special accent, and give a gift to those forgotten corners of your dwelling and to yourself.

hello, yellow

YELLOW GLOWS, AS IF THE COLOR ITSELF WERE A SOURCE OF POWER. It's not just the sun in the morning. It is also the color of our favorite flowers, the tartness of lemons, a bright finch, a symbol of wealth in the form of gold, a campfire at night, a field of dandelions, or the center of a fried egg.

Buddhist monks wear saffron robes; to them, the color represents wisdom, concentration, knowledge, and morality. To chromopaths (those New Age docs who use color to heal), yellow is the Ritalin of colors because it's stimulating to adults and soothing to children. But natural healers also recognize yellow as the color of awareness and sometimes use it to treat memory loss.

To color guru Faber Birren, yellow not only had a visual power but also sounded like French horns; to Isaac Newton, it was equivalent to an E note on the music scale. There is only one song I know of that really honors this glorious color; written by flower child Donovan in the 1960s,

it convinced a generation that yellow was "mellow"—quite rightly.

Feng shui practitioners also believe that yellow is mellow. They consider certain shades of yellow—especially earthy yellows, such as ochre—to represent tranquillity, meditation, and strength in reserve. And it was an important color in the mysterious operations of Middle Age alchemists.

Considering all this symbolic history, it's somewhat odd that yellow has come to represent cowardice. But it's no mystery as to why highway hazard signs, school buses, police crime-scene tape, taxicabs, and traffic-cop raincoats are yellow: Yellow is the color most easily seen during daylight.

That's also why yellow is favored for consumer-goods packaging. (Although in the consumer arena, yellow is perceived as being cheap. So it's good for potato chips, but not so good for caviar.)

To modern-day color psychologists, yellow is relaxed and optimistic. I agree. I personally like the red-casted yellows best. I like the zones on the color wheel where yellow drifts into pumpkin, mango, and saffron, where the yellows have a rich warmth, and I love the way they coordinate with both cool and warm colors. Whenever I bring those kinds of yellows into a room, the mood becomes comfortable, cheerful, and enriching—just like the warmth of the sun.

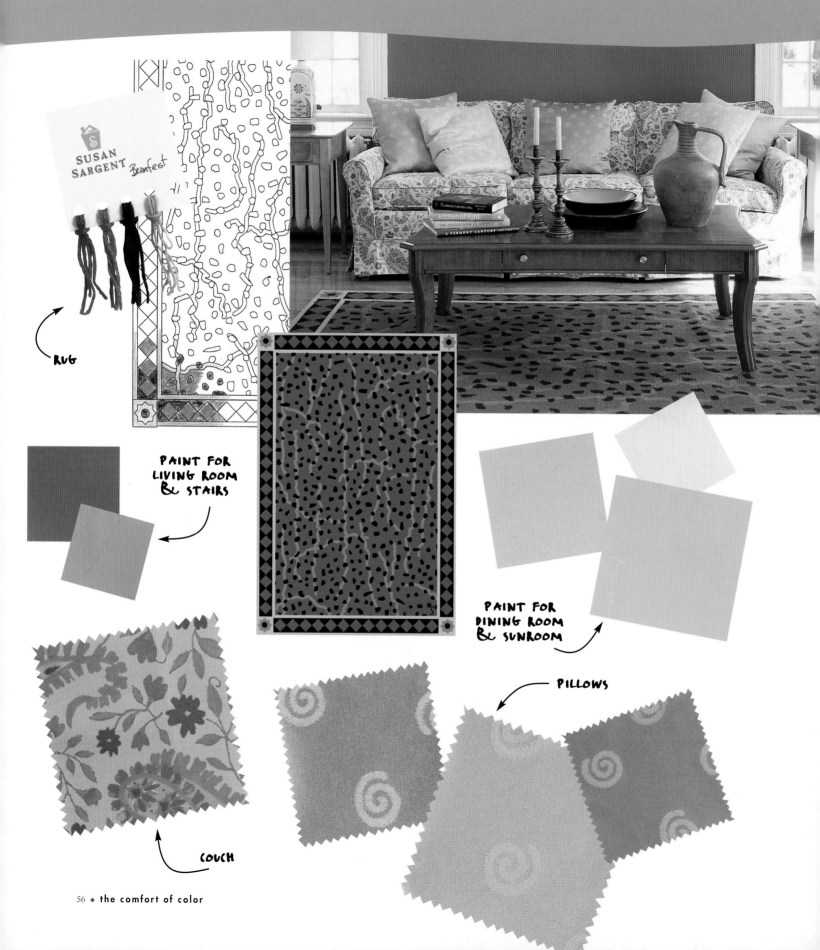

SUSAN SARGENT *Bearfest*

RUG

PAINT FOR LIVING ROOM & STAIRS

PAINT FOR DINING ROOM & SUNROOM

PILLOWS

COUCH

PAINT FOR
CLOSET

PAINT FOR
MASTER
BEDROOM

RUG

SUSAN
SARGENT   Pop

PAINT FOR
GUEST ROOM

WALL HANGING

CURTAINS

BEDSPREAD

CHAIR

CURTAINS

the tao of decorating ◆ 57

no room is an island

I've never lived in a railroad flat. But I know people who have, and nowhere is there a better illustration of how color choices can turn a bunch of unrelated rooms into a smooth and beautiful suite.

In case you've forgotten, a railroad flat is an apartment or house that's long and narrow, with rooms that are strung together, front to back, like train cars. The first room is the living room, with windows facing the street. A bedroom (or two) leads to the dining room, followed by the kitchen "caboose"—last in line but blessed with backyard windows. Nobody builds that type of railroad flat anymore. They're thought of as urban mistakes, the by-products of ill-conceived subdivisions or overcrowded worker housing.

For our purposes, however, the railroad flat is a valuable model because it reminds us that every room—no matter where it's positioned—is a link in a chain. It is a mistake to think about the redecoration of one room without considering the rooms that surround

Pale yellow walls segue to marmalade and then orange as the three front rooms are linked by a progression of color.

the lady and the light

Stephanie Hynds has lived in places where color is color. As a graduate student, she studied storytelling in Indonesia and West Africa; as a working actress, she spent ten years in Southern California.

She's been on tropical islands where jungle foliage presses against buildings and roads, where blossoms, birds, and butterflies draw attention to themselves with the intense hues of their petals and wings. In Los Angeles, sunshine and irrigation ensure views of tall palms, green grass, fruit trees, and flowers that can't help but grow.

Still, glorious color, balmy weather, and excellent produce weren't enough to keep her there. Stephanie and her husband, Stan, craved the drama of four distinct seasons and wanted a close-knit community in which to raise a family. So they returned to the East Coast and bought a Cape-style house in New England.

Relocation was not easy with Wally, then a toddler, in tow. The couple rented for the first few years and finally bought a small, traditional Cape, built in the 1970s but subsequently painted dispiriting shades of brown and gray. Stan, Stephanie, and Wally moved in on the eve of the birth of their second child, Florrie, and it was some time before they could get their heads above water to even notice their surroundings, let alone finish unpacking their boxes.

One day last November, with their fourth winter approaching, Stephanie came up for air and realized she was color-deprived. "I looked outside and there was nothing," she told me. "The sky was white, there were no leaves on the trees, no grass on the ground, no color at all."

INSPIRATION

ABOVE: Stephanie trained in Indonesia to use these classic shadow puppets, made of painted tin. Each one symbolizes a different traditional god or story.

OPPOSITE: Florrie and Wally try out their new playroom, under the bemused gaze of the Bard.

it. The dining room is in cahoots with the kitchen; the bathroom has a shy alliance with the hallway. As you walk from the living room to the kitchen to get a snack, the whole of your home can—and should—unfold before you: each space with its own personality, of course, yet splashed with integrated colors that are glimpsed through doorways and reach around corners in a sympathetic harmony.

OPPOSITE: Primary
colors can be used artfully
and well without being
childish. This room
welcomes children as
well as their parents.

ABOVE: An antique
theater from Stephanie's
childhood.

She couldn't control the landscape—which
does have its own subtle beauty in November—
but she could offset it with color in her home.
Stephanie took control of her interior life. She
decided she wanted "passion" colors for the
house and found inspiration in her collection
of Indonesian shadow puppets, which had
been tucked away in the attic for safekeeping.
They brought her mind and eye back to a
place where textiles are dyed with thrilling
hues, bright birds perch on bright flowers, and
warm island markets are laden with bright
fruits. No matter what the weather outside,
she would have color and excitement inside.

the skinny house

Turn the railroad flat sideways. Give it an old-fashioned garden with a picket fence out front, and set it down in a small town. Give it a linear layout with a sweep from left to right: living room, foyer, dining room, family room, guest room, deck. To every room add lots of windows that face both directions, for maximum light and solar gain. Build a kitchen and bathroom off the back, add a second floor, and you've got the "Skinny House." If you stand at one end, you can look through doorways all the way down to the other end, catching glimpses of angles and walls all the way through. (And if you're a child, you can have endless and irresistible fun galloping back and forth.)

My goal for Stephanie and Stan's Skinny House was to help them bring the house alive, building a connected color story that flowed from one end to the other. By day, it would be a gleeful home in constant motion. By night, it would be a richly hued retreat in which to read, dine, converse, and play music in different, colorful zones.

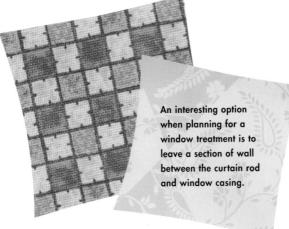

An interesting option when planning for a window treatment is to leave a section of wall between the curtain rod and window casing.

We began with the living room. This was Stephanie and Stan's least favorite area, primarily because it was painted with a depressing brownish color that reminded Stan of "a wet Band-Aid." Yet it should have been cozy, with a fireplace at one end and windows on two sides.

Our point of departure was a new slipcover for the sofa. Stephanie had chosen it because it combined her desire for warm passion colors with an easy, Scandinavian-style print. "I've been a flaming liberal in every respect but decorating," she confessed. "I like old houses and antiques and, until recently, very traditional colors." The fabric suited both her past and current tastes and gave the room a clear direction.

The living room was crying out for boldness. My color team and I looked at their art, their Indonesian collections, and their favorite flowers. Ultimately, a wonderful burnt orange replaced the dismal Band-Aid brown. Two mission-style leather chairs, which Stephanie described as "black holes," got recovered in a pale green matelassé. Light cotton curtains with a delicate print, and a layer of whitewash over the liver-colored brick fireplace balanced

MIX AND MATCH: Once a rich orange replaced the "wet Band-Aid" color in the living room, the disparate elements found a happy coexistence.

The reupholstered mission-style furniture mixes peacefully with the floral couch, while simple cotton curtains in a country style let in lots of light.

frame shop

IN THE BACK CORNER OF STEPHANIE AND STAN'S LIVING ROOM IS AN OPENING TO A SMALL HALL. This little space doesn't have much to do but provide a route to their home office and a shortcut to the back door. A person wouldn't give it much notice, but when Stephanie and Stan's living room was painted, that little opening looked shadowy and peculiar. It didn't look, in fact, as if it belonged to this newly glowing house at all. We didn't want to distract from the glorious orange living room walls by straying too far in color, so we wallpapered the hall with a subtle tone-on-tone pattern that made it an extension of the main room.

The hallway now looked as though it belonged. But on the one-thing-leads-to-another principle, the stark white door trim now seemed wrong. Door casings are wonderful little opportunities to use a color you don't want too much of, which can surprise or amuse you or simply enhance whatever lies beyond. We painted a lovely glossy soft lime around the opening, which defined and framed the inner hall and the tiny table and lamp that stood there.

If we call this little trick "framing," it would be pretty accurate. It's about painting a contrasting color on a section of trim in order to set off the "view" in the next room, while highlighting the trim itself. Virtually any type of decorative element—window sashes, baseboards, crown molding, chair rails, or wainscoting—can be painted to make a room more interesting.

the saturated walls. Accent pillows and a vibrant rug with related color fields pulled all the elements together.

If you walk from the living room to the dining room, you pass by the front door on your right and look up the stairway to your left, pausing in a little hall. We redid this entryway to link all three spaces. In the adjoining dining room, the trim was already a soft blue-green, which we all liked. We sweetened the white walls to the color of ripe mangoes and hung two-tone draperies in mango and sunshine in a lustrous fabric. A set of flea-market chairs were painted in lime, periwinkle, teal, and blueberry, and the classic ironwork chandelier got new shades in mango and red.

Continuing on our stroll, we step down into the family room, officially used for music and play. But with plain white walls, brown floor, brown piano, and blank windows, it didn't look like much fun to me. Children's energy needs color energy to back it up. Mindful of the links-in-a-chain approach necessary to a railroad house, we shifted gently from dining-room mango to a softer sunny yellow, with a second lemony paint tone for an angled wall along the ceiling.

As a mother, I know that floors belong to children. The floor is their playground, their dreamscape, their domain. The family room, with great light on both sides, seemed a perfect place for a brightly colored painted floor. We chose a high-gloss spring green, which drew the kids like a magnet and brought the outdoors in, all year-round. I dislike wall-to-wall carpeting—probably because 90 percent of it is beige or white—so on the new bright floor we laid cheerful rugs

that provided different zones for child play.

Through another door, another step, and a guest suite of bed and bath, we slide into a quieter zone, and we used softer blues and greens instead of primaries, with fuchsia accents in the bedcovering, curtains, and window-seat fabric.

upstairs, downstairs

In contrast to all the heat on the first floor, the stairwell and upstairs hall were made over in blues and light greens. The staircase wall has a dividing beam above the handrail, which, now painted a violet blue, draws the eye up the stairs to the hall above, where blue-striped wallpaper is just visible in the upstairs bathroom. A lively runner, also patterned in blues and greens, dances up the stairs.

Virtually the only room untouched by color in Stephanie and Stan's home was their first-floor kitchen, which is still dominated by the original weathered barnboard cabinetry. A novelty back in the 1970s, today the look has fallen out of favor and is downright depressing against the playful walls and floors. Stephanie is shopping for paint that will wake her kitchen up, yet harmonize with the other colors in her skinny house. "I'm definitely going to be more bold," she said. "I'll make mistakes, but I don't care. I was living in a black-and-white movie; now, my life is in color."

"I'm definitely going to be more bold. I'll make mistakes, but I don't care."

—STEPHANIE HYNDS

Shades of honey, lemon, and marmalade fill the dining room. The lustrous fabric in the curtains shimmers on a sunny alfresco lunch.

where chromophobia meets homophobia

STEPHANIE AND STAN SLEEP ACROSS THE HALL FROM THEIR TWO CHILDREN, in a room with an irregular shape and the sloped ceiling typical of Cape-style houses. It will become their daughter's room once she is older. Meanwhile, it seemed like the right idea to paint it a saturated raspberry in advance. The effect was gorgeous, but Stan wasn't amused.

He's no color prude: he had rolled right along with every other transformation in the house, including the radical flourish of glossy green paint on the family room floor. Of that, he'd said, "It's so crazy, it just might work."

But raspberry walls were not okay for his bedroom. Please know that Stan is among the most enlightened of males—the most enlightened of humans, for that matter. Thoughtful and literary, he is untouched by macho posturings and doesn't have a sexist molecule in his brain or body. But when I pressed him about his reason for disliking the raspberry bedroom, he balked, made excuses, and then came clean: "It's pink," he said.

Pink is where chromophobia meets homophobia. Of all the colors in the spectrum, pink is by far the most gender-charged, and most heterosexual men—no matter how evolved they might be—reject it automatically. (Stan has plenty of company: when I was thinking of repainting our own bedroom, my husband, Tom—also an

enlightened New Age guy in most ways—said, "Fine—anything but pink.") It's not a wholesale damnation of the color itself. They probably love it in its place—on their wives and daughters, in raspberry sherbet and strawberry daiquiris, and in Bermuda. And oddly enough, it seems to be perfectly okay in the country club world for men to wear pink cardigans, linen jackets, and pants—even for guys who would be appalled to be called anything but Men. But don't even think about bringing it onto their walls. Especially their bedroom walls.

It's an obvious, learned bias. In our culture, pink has been entirely appropriated by females. The affiliation begins at birth, when, indisputably, little pink blankets are for girls, and baby blue is for boys. But boys' exclusive alliance with blue fades by the age of three or so. Walk through the boys' aisles at Toys "R" Us and you'll see a riot of conflicting colors—army green, gunmetal gray, Tonka truck yellow, fire engine red.

Round the corner into the girls' section and you'll be blinded by pink. It's not just the products—doll dresses, plastic ponies, tea sets, tricycles—it's also the packaging. Little girls appear to be born with a powerful attachment to pink, which marketing gurus and the "pink-is-for-girls" association constantly support by endless varieties of toys, dolls, clothing, board books, and even a new line of pink Legos.

Pink options for females soon shift from pink fairies to lipstick, from princesses to peonies, from ballet shoes to high heels. But the average male is never invited into this club, and only the most intrepid will cross the line and choose rose over "sweatshirt gray."

Of course, not all women like pink, either, rejecting it for its girlie stereotype as much as for its garish interpretation. I have never felt any attraction myself for the fluffy bubblegum pinks that reign in retail stores, although I am entranced by any pink found in my garden—the palest peach, the most

delicate rose, any of the pinky lavenders and raspberry peonies.

Would Stan have rejected the raspberry bedroom without the cultural biases we have had bred into us?

In all fairness to Stan, the color was also rejected by Stephanie. The deep color seemed to suck up sunlight, becoming almost black after nightfall. Stephanie repainted the room in a tulip

red that complemented the bedspread, and both she and Stan are happy with the new color. Though still rich and romantic, the room doesn't disappear in the dark. And it's no longer pink.

OPPOSITE: The guest room design was created around a hooked rug. Fuchsia, soft green, reds, and blues combine in assorted accents.

ABOVE: In the adjoining bathroom, the tiles and wall color extend the color story.

LEFT: Stephanie's grandmother's chair waits for bedtime readings.

working notes

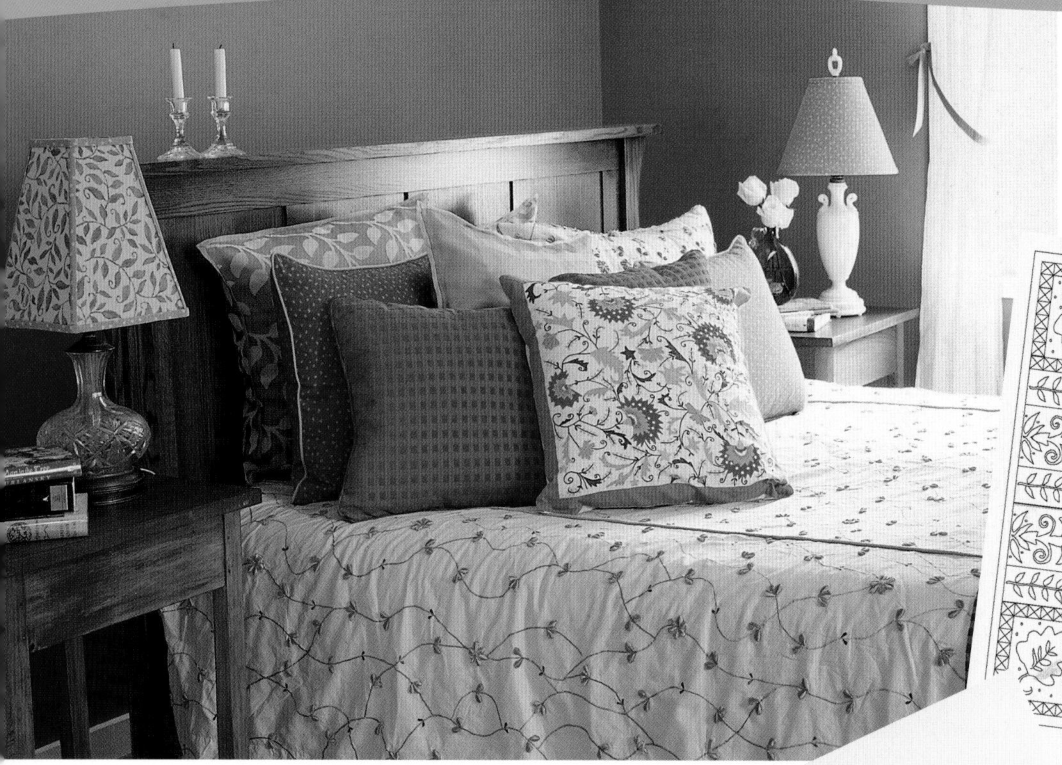

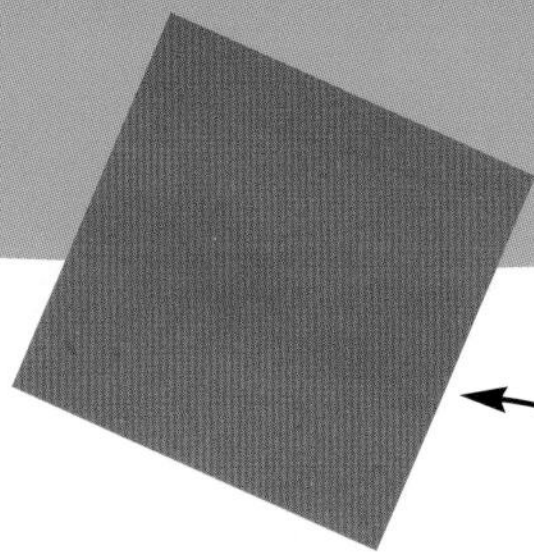

PAINT FOR BEDROOM

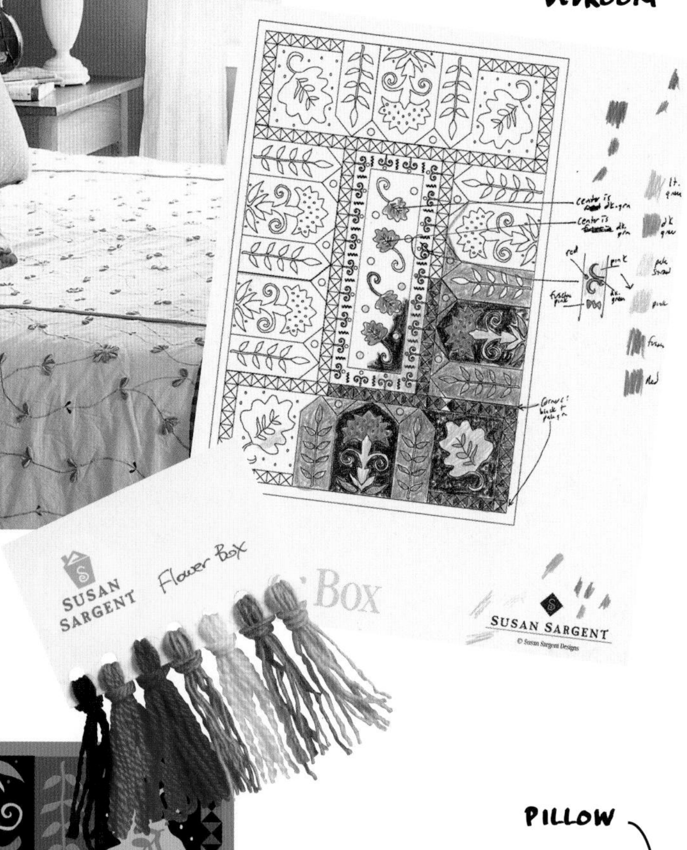

SUSAN SARGENT
Flower Box
Box
SUSAN SARGENT
© Susan Sargent Designs

PILLOW

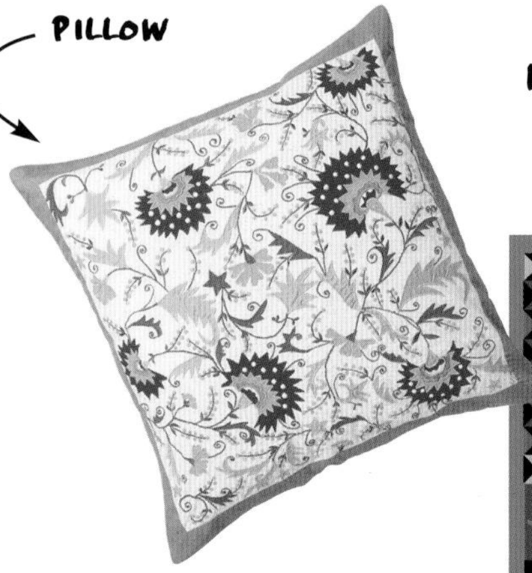

RUG

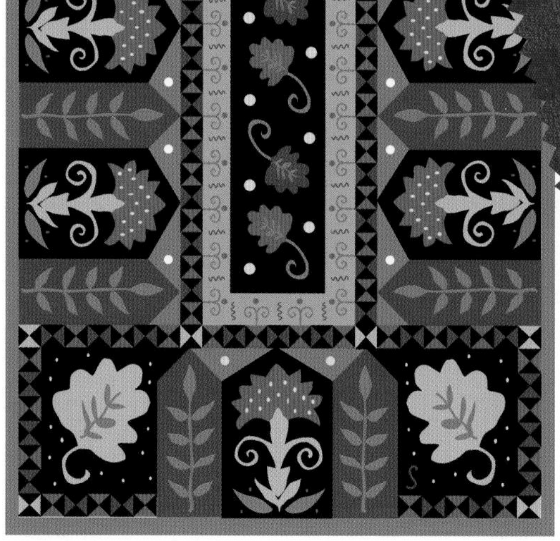

PILLOW

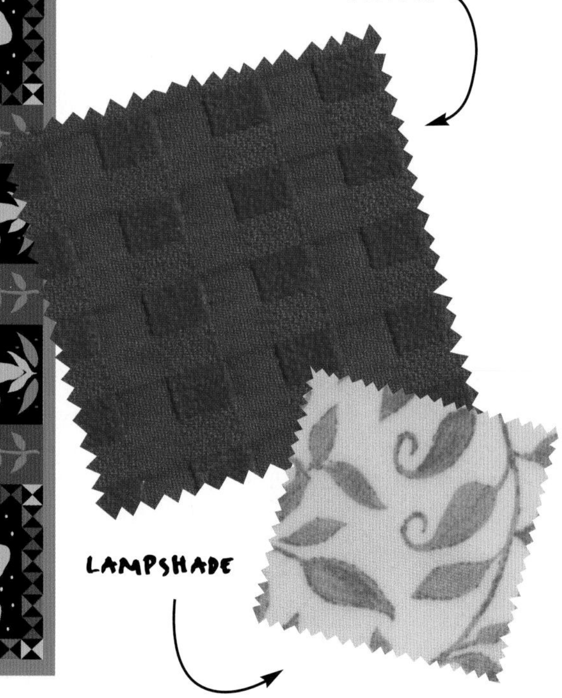

PAINT FOR MUSIC ROOM

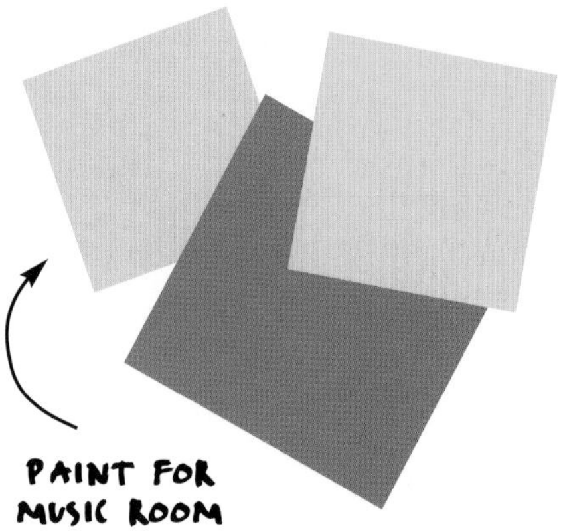

LAMPSHADE

PAINT FOR
DINING ROOM

FLEA MARKET
CHAIRS FRESHLY
PAINTED

CHANDELIER

TABLECLOTH

CURTAINS

RUG

SUSAN SARGENT Plaid Dk

PAINT FOR
STAIRWAY/HALL

PAINT FOR
LIVING ROOM

CHAPTER 4

this old house, these new colors

QUESTION: What happens when an old house filled with antiques gets a dose of contemporary color?

ANSWER: It looks better, fresher, and younger. It loses its fustiness without losing its place in history. It reflects its owners' modern sensibilities while still respecting their love of tradition.

Nancy and Paul Schwindt know this well. Twenty years ago, they bought a fine old house with high ceilings and classic proportions. It needed work, but between Paul's architectural savvy and Nancy's decorating talents, the couple soon turned the 1814 structure into a home for their children and a showplace in which to entertain friends.

Furnished, for the most part, with pieces inherited from Paul's family, the house boasted a grand piano, formal foyer, banquet-size dining table with built-in cabinetry, custom drapes, and perfectly framed fireplaces.

BREAKING WITH TRADITION: This sunny breakfast table is in a corner of the newly remodeled kitchen. Antique chairs with fabric seats paired with a bright floral rug tie it all together.

At about the time her two children became teenagers, Nancy painted the living room red. Not *red,* as in Chinese lucky numbers, cardinal feathers, or Santa Claus suits, but "red," as in a warm but subdued color that was historically appropriate. She also glazed the dining-room walls with subtle stripes.

Both rooms looked lovely, but there was a formality about the place that didn't suit the couple. They were more prone to Rollerblading and mountain biking than hosting proper tea parties with elderly patrons of the arts. With these activities, they spent a good portion of their time escaping their proper, upright home.

a wing and a prayer

Nancy and Paul didn't become one with their space until they redesigned the kitchen and mudroom, the back wing of their home, to create a big open kitchen with a fireplace on the gable wall. New cabinetry in the cooking area utilized ancient boards rescued from the house's attic. The space had windows on three sides and had room for both dining and lounging.

To create her seating area in front of the fireplace, Nancy recruited a century-old couch that had once belonged to Paul's grandmother. "When we got it, it was covered in a quilted chintz that belonged in Palm Beach," she said. She added two formal upholstered armchairs for additional seating. Seeking a look that was in tune with the new wing's comfortable atmosphere, she surprised herself by choosing fabrics from my Grover Farm collection that were as relaxed as a pair of jeans. The sofa, retaining its classic shape and its carved mahogany legs, became jazzy and casual in periwinkle blue. The Queen Anne armchairs, with rolled arms and claw-feet,

color as emotional sanctuary

SOMETIMES PEOPLE NEED TO DRAW THEIR DWELLINGS AROUND THEM LIKE A BLANKET AND FIND SOLACE THERE. When Nancy and Paul extended their kitchen and added a colorful sitting room, it immediately became the heart of their home. Then Nancy lost her thirty-five-year-old sister to cancer, and that cluster of bright furniture around the fireplace became much more than a pretty place to sit; it became her shelter from the storm. "I spent most of that winter on this couch," Nancy recalled. "It was a place of total comfort. When I was away, dealing with the family and my nephews, at some point I'd say, 'I've got to go home to the blue couch.' "

To her, that sofa was the essence of home, an antidote to the other kind of "blues." The colors that surround it—clear indigo, bright greens, touches of yellow and magenta, by far the liveliest hues in her house—also had a positive effect on her emotions. "They're cheerful, comforting, and uplifting," she said.

Color psychologists are in her corner. They've learned that for most people, blue is calming, yellow is optimistic, and green is inspiring. Feng shui practitioners teach that both blue and green enhance harmony and growth. These beliefs run right up against another piece of conventional wisdom: that people who are upset should be kept quiet in body and mind, shielded from all but the blandest and most calming environments.

The idea that vivid colors in appealing doses would deepen the pain of someone in distress is an odd one to me. The chilling monotony of an all-white box would push most of us closer to despair than any well-thought-out color scheme. Nancy's comfort in her bright room supports my own fervent conviction that colors offer solace in inexplicable but real ways.

Color fanatics past and present have many theories about color and mood. One Web site declares that "drab and dingy colors harm our spirits" and that "if we use [colors] intelligently they can help us by strengthening, soothing, and inspiring us."

Unfortunately, colors can't heal a broken heart or even a broken toe. But they can soothe us while we recover, be a solace for the eye while the rest of us is aching, and remind us of things we treasure and find joy in, beyond the bounds of our own sadness.

"Colors offer solace in inexplicable but real ways."

could have been covered with toile or brocade to look right at home in a formal parlor. Instead, Nancy reupholstered them in a lustrous bright green fabric, the shade of a just-picked Granny Smith apple.

"These were breakthrough colors for me," admitted Nancy. "At first, they were a bit of a shock for both of us." Centered on a vibrant rug in front of the fireplace, the grouping quickly took on a life of its own and became the family's favorite gathering place.

In fact, the room became so popular that the couple's big house had effectively turned into a small house. "The living room is good for opening presents at Christmas, but this is where we live," said Paul of the new edition. "The rest of the house is almost superfluous."

dreamy to dreary, and back again

There was a time when Nancy and Paul thought their house *was* colorful. But their bright and friendly makeover set the bar higher for using color. "I saw the light when we did this room," said Nancy. "My eye got adjusted." Because of the Schwindts' newfound color vision, other rooms in the house began looking woefully faded. The master bedroom, in particular, looked like a ghost from another era. Decorated with a Laura Ashley–type palette, the room had cream-colored walls, off-white wall-to-wall carpeting, and elaborate draperies in a cabbage rose print. "At the time we did it, I thought my bedroom looked dreamy," recalled Nancy. "Then the downstairs was done, and those cabbage roses started bringing me down."

She and Paul dragged one of my high-impact rugs upstairs and put it on their bedroom floor. "We're ripping up the beige

OPPOSITE: These good antique chairs used to be invisible, covered in a dull "historic" fabric. They acquired a new appeal and a new outfit, soft lime with a spiral woven pattern.

ABOVE: A vibrant checkers game and mosaic vase complement the reupholstered furniture.

the power of blue

WE SING THE BLUES AND WE FEEL THE BLUES. Blue is dark, the color of melancholy and gloom. Yet blue can also be upbeat and is many people's favorite color, particularly for bedrooms. It has had emotional and symbolic meanings across different cultures and throughout the centuries.

BLUE FACTS

◆ Among chromopaths—that is, those who heal with color—blue is believed to lower blood pressure and help cure insomnia, hypertension, and nervousness. As the ultimate sleep color, it is called upon to slow the pulse and increase dream activity. As the color of truth, it is believed to strengthen intuition and psychic powers and create clear channels to the spiritual self.

◆ The blue of indigo dye is supposed to be irresistible to mosquitoes. But medium blue paint was used to repel flies in the Deep South.

◆ Blue represented piety and sincerity in European heraldry; truth for the ancient Druids; mercy in the Kabbalah; and the Virgin Mary for Catholics. And in voodoo, blue is for protection and peace.

◆ In Boston, blue bloods are socially prominent, blue laws enforce moral codes, and blue movies are X-rated.

◆ Venus's color is blue-green, and Neptune's is indigo.

◆ Krishna is blue, and for Sikhs, a blue turban indicates a mind that is as broad as the sky.

◆ Blue stands for the direction north for the Sioux, for the direction south in Tibet.

◆ In 1908 the theosophist Annie Besant stated that "the different shades of blue all indicate religious feeling, and range through all hues from the dark brown-blue of selfish devotion, or the pallid grey-blue of fetish-worship tinged with fear, up to the rich deep clear colour of heartfelt adoration, and the beautiful pale azure of that highest form which implies self-renunciation and union with the divine."

◆ The painter Wassily Kandinsky had a particular liking for blue and assigned it doses of spirituality. "The deeper the blue becomes, the more strongly it calls man toward the infinite. . . . Blue is the typical heavenly colour. Blue unfolds in its lowest depths the element of tranquility. As it deepens towards black, it assumes overtones of a superhuman sorrow. . . . The Brighter it becomes, the more it loses its sounds and turns into silent stillness."

◆ Kandinsky was musical, too, and played the cello. His blues also had positions in his musical hierarchy. "Represented in musical terms, light blue resembles the flute, dark blue the cello, darker still the wonderful sounds of the double bass, while in the deep, solemn form the sound of blue can be compared to that of the deep tones of the organ."

I am in love with blue, returning to it endlessly in my work. I am drawn toward the red-casted blues—periwinkle, violet, and lavender. Certain blues have color associations for me that no doubt affect my choices, and blue flowers of all types are continual inspiration.

Perhaps my favorite blue is the color of twilight, that certain shade that appears between day and night when the sky drifts from cerulean to midnight and for a time settles on a violet blue that adds and subtracts light, in equal measure. An infinite mix, alive with possibilities.

OPPOSITE: A view looking from the new kitchen to the original part of the house, now a home office and television room. The back wall has been covered in a Japanese material.
ABOVE: The classic front entry hall and main staircase, where traditional toile wallpaper is at home with a modern carpet.

carpet, putting in a dark floor, and decorating the room with exciting colors," said Nancy. "Those floral drapes are about to be history."

Today, the couple is looking at other ways to ratchet up color in the rest of their house. They cherish its history, its flow, its shape, and its scale. They remain true to the charm of the perfect bones of the house. But they have come to realize that there is more than one way to honor an architectural gem. They are giving their house a new launch into another century, filling it with life and the power of color.

THIS PAGE: The girls' pretty bathroom has a classic tub and airy floral curtain.
OPPOSITE: Daughter Alexa chose the soft apricot walls for her bedroom and gave pink a hip new identity.

working notes

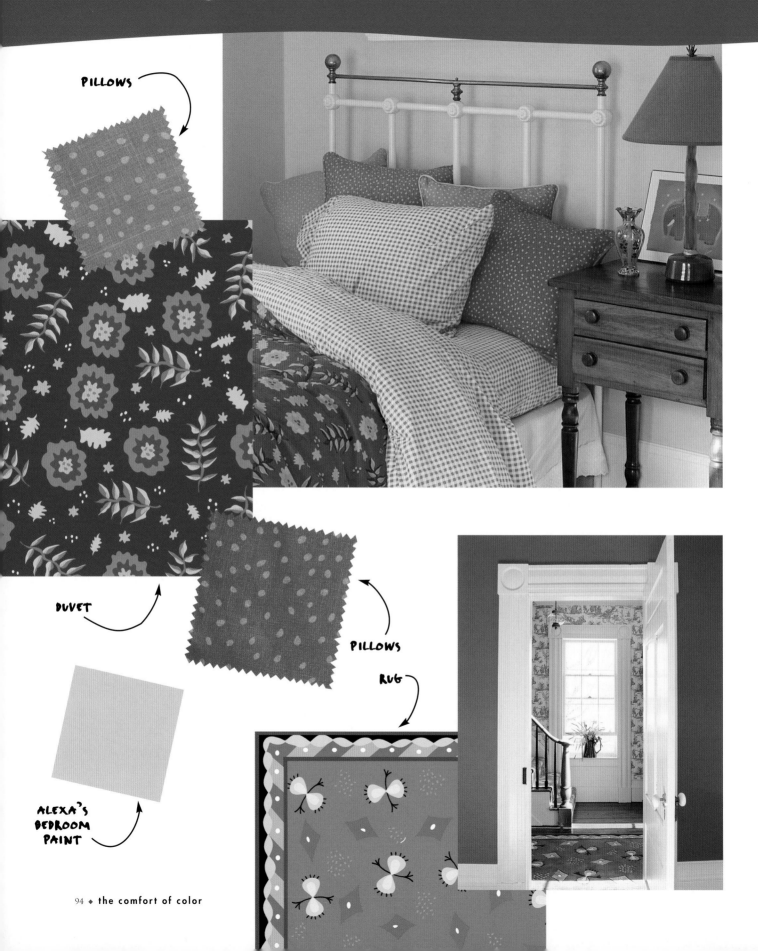

PILLOWS

DUVET

PILLOWS

RUG

ALEXA'S
BEDROOM
PAINT

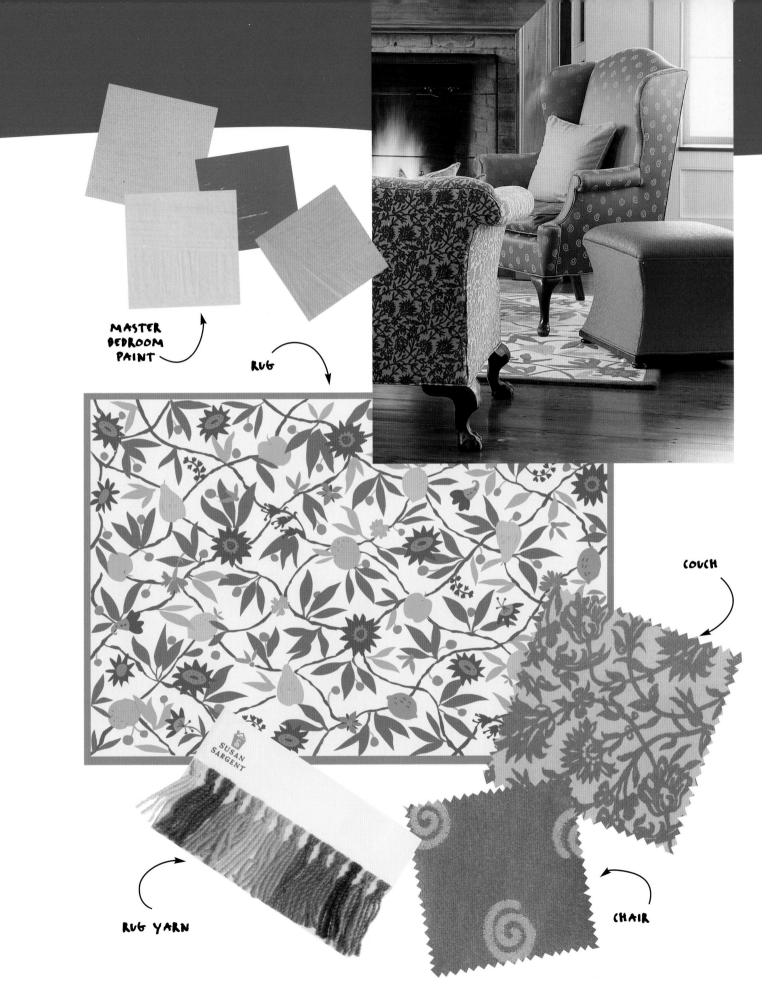

MASTER
BEDROOM
PAINT

RUG

COUCH

RUG YARN

CHAIR

SUSAN
SARGENT

from shack to shelter

The tiny house clings to the edge of the road near the center of a small village. Out-of-towners speeding by would never suspect that the cottage is nearly two hundred years old and that it once served as a shed for horse-drawn buggies. Nor might they notice that at its back an open deck cantilevers over the millpond, where a decisive battle of the Revolutionary War was fought.

In the 1890s the structure was sound and sturdy. A century later, it had devolved into a wreck that seemed fated to collapse under the weight of weather and neglect. It had been open to the elements, it was windowless . . . but it wasn't quite a teardown. "It still had a lot of charm," said its owner, John Teaford.

John, who has spent much of his life traveling the world as a speed skater, Olympic coach, and extreme-sports filmmaker, bought the property in 2000. His outdoor experience came in handy as he bivouacked while restoring the building, added a second-story sleeping loft under its rafters, and moved in.

John is his family's historian and keeper of the family archive. A banner from his grandfather's Adirondack camp hangs in the living room. The floors and much of the woodwork were left natural, while the bookshelves and trim board got a touch of paint to break up the unrelenting brown.

ABOVE: The green bookcase is filled with well-read volumes, interspersed with objets dear to the couple's hearts. The green repeats on the shutters (opposite) that open onto the sleeping loft.

RIGHT: The antique horns were mounted on an orange beam above the door into the kitchen in this Scandinavian-feel cottage.

The walls were now stark white. The woodwork, doors, and floors were plain brown wood. Most of the furniture was brown wood and brown leather. Sports gear lined the entry, and sports photos hung on the walls. Though clean and perfectly tidy, it was clear that no womanly hand had been involved. A "guy"—the literary and thoughtful version, but still "a guy"—lived here.

John unpacked long-stored books, family heirlooms, black-and-white photos, and mementos gathered during his travels. "I was in danger of becoming a hermit in my book-lined cave," he admitted.

breakfast with tiffany

Enter Tiffany Beck, another former professional athlete and refugee from the road. She and John first met in 1997, but the two didn't lock eyes until five years later. By then, Tiffany had retired from the national circuit, in which she had distinguished herself as a cross-country skier and bike racer. Like John, she was a transient creature: sports and travel came first, and she had "never had a home to put stuff in." Unlike John, she had never been a pack rat and could "fit [her] belongings in six duffel bags and move in two days." The two athletes became engaged, and she moved in to John's bachelor cottage, with those six bags plus the skis and bicycles that were her primary possessions.

Other women might have been daunted by the limitations of a three-room cottage, even without the challenge of moving in to one already stuffed to the rafters. Yet she was determined to put her own stamp on their home, and John was fully supportive. "It's no longer just my house. It's ready to be shared,"

he said. "If there are six pictures on the wall, two should be hers, two should be mine, and two should be ours."

Tiff admittedly had no decorating experience—"My idea of decorating hadn't gotten past a pinecone and a hurricane lamp"—but she is hugely sensitive to color and has visceral and specific feelings about different shades. The colors she is most comfortable with are natural colors from the outdoors—greens, yellows, blues, and oranges from the quieter side of the scale—with accents of bright color sprinkled like wildflowers in a meadow.

john faces his color fears

Tiff recruited me to work with them on the color makeover, but John was cautious. He had always chosen white walls as a serene background for his black-and-white photographs and his creative musings. One of his worries was that an active, colorful space might be a distraction. "I'm always working in my head," he said. "I worried that color inside the house would be more of a challenge than a comfort to me."

He also feared that the little cottage would fall victim to the "Hansel and Gretel Syndrome." Despite his affinity for Scandinavia and the Alps, he was well aware of the fine line between charming and cutesy. He was getting married, but he wasn't ready to live in a candy shop.

inspiration

Wearing my color therapist hat, I spent time with John and Tiff, looking at fabrics and colors and listening to them talk things through. Tiff had fallen for a flowery fabric that had paprika

The rustic cottage avoids cuteness with a judicious mix of antiques, natural wood, and Scandinavian colors. A vintage Swedish wall cabinet hangs above the living-room daybed.

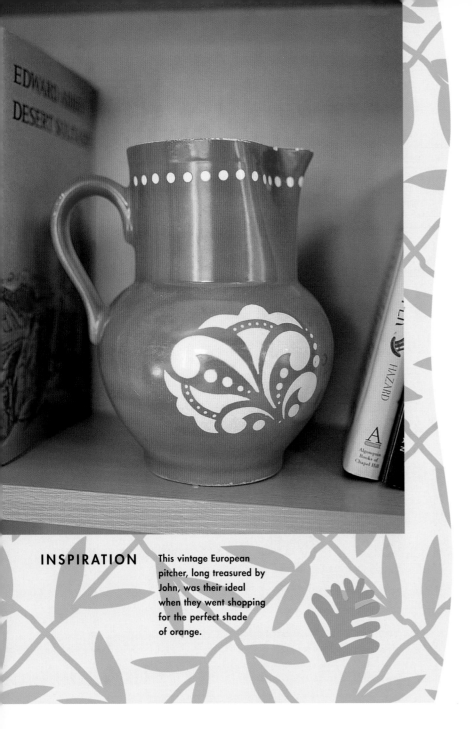

INSPIRATION This vintage European pitcher, long treasured by John, was their ideal when they went shopping for the perfect shade of orange.

John's comfort level was greatly increased when he thought of painting test boards before beginning the real thing. Being able to see a bigger patch—he used a 3' x 6" board for each color—was just what he needed, and he was able to adjust the colors to a point where he found them harmonious. (Incidentally, they were also very Scandinavian.)

Now things really started to move. Compromises were reached on how much of the woodwork would be painted in the soft green—the bookcases and the interior shutters, yes. All the other trim and windows, no. And both agreed to match the pitcher's red-orange on a horizontal beam that bisected the living-room walls about halfway up. (The accent paint closest to the pitcher was called fireball orange, and John recalls being questioned by an incredulous clerk: You want *how* much of *what* color?)

Yet despite its name, fireball orange was a pleasant hue, not fluorescent and just the shade of certain autumn leaves at their most brilliant in the fall. The orange beam became a linear display board, on which John mounted an unusual collection of roebuck horns (ca. 1912) that he'd inherited from an eccentric great-aunt.

Several Scandinavian blues picked out the kitchen cupboards and the staircase risers and continued up to the sleeping loft. At the very top of the staircase, a deep blue cupboard under the eaves was a pleasant visual surprise.

Upstairs in the sleeping loft, the newly painted shutters open onto a bird's-eye view of the living room. John, by now getting in stride with the transformation, agreed to "temporarily" paint the bedroom's gable wall the same fireball orange. The floor in the

and soft green designs on a butter-colored background. John took a deep breath—he had wooden shutters instead of curtains—but became comfortable with the concept when he realized that the paprika color in the fabric was an exact match for a treasured antique pitcher. The pitcher had pride of place on the living-room shelf and became the reference point for choosing a coordinating blue, a yellow, and a green.

getting started:
the tie and scarf strategy

MANY PEOPLE WANT TO START
SMALL WITH COLOR, BUILDING THEIR
CONFIDENCE AS THEY GO ALONG. I
find it helps to think of that approach
as the scarf and tie strategy. It's a lot
easier to be adventurous with a
bright scarf or a snappy tie than to
step out on impulse in a traffic-
stopping outfit. Tiff's wardrobe sticks
to earth tones or black generally, but
she uses scarves to add life to a
humdrum outfit.

The nice thing about this approach is
its flexibility. You don't have to make
a huge commitment, and can exchange
one bright accent for another with the
flick of a wrist. Whether it's a scarf,
a vivid pillow, a small accent rug, a
painted table, or a lampshade, this is
a great way to change your mood in
an instant and begin to get familiar
with the way colors make you feel and
how you want to mix them up.

**The narrow living room,
once a sea of brown,
now accommodates the
tastes and color interests
of both residents.**

on orange

THERE'S SOMETHING TRAGIC ABOUT ORANGE. Not the color, which I love, and certainly not the fruit, which I also love. It's the word *orange* that causes problems. It's a great example of how language fails to describe color. Legendary colorist Josef Albers once stated that the "nomenclature of color is most inadequate." And orange is probably the most misunderstood of all.

I find the range of oranges to be among the most beautiful for home furnishings. I don't mean orange as in plastic pumpkins, Kool-Aid, iMacs, and Home Depot signs. They fall under the umbrella name, too, but orange is big enough to cover an enormous range of gorgeous colors, including paprika, terra-cotta, amber, marigold, burnt orange, passion, salmon, marmalade, and flame.

But I have bowed to cultural biases and associations and have learned to avoid using the word in presenting an idea for interior color. Say "orange" and people see either the roof of a Howard Johnson motor lodge or the color of a clown's wig, and they are not inspired by the thought. Stick to the *real* words, words like *saffron, persimmon, cider, cinnamon,* and *russet* and the reception is always positive. Poor orange (the word) is misunderstood.

THIS PAGE: Collections of shells and arrowheads, along with vintage curiosities, add an original touch to the interior.

OPPOSITE: Scandinavian blue defines the simple cottage kitchen.

loft was plywood. After a few coats of shiny yellow paint and a couple of nice small rugs, it became radiant, and the light from the river below reflected off the sunny, glossy surface. A pretty floral bedcover and some patterned cotton curtains upstairs satisfied Tiff that she was there to stay.

afterglow

Within the course of a few furious days, John's bachelor home was transformed into a cheerful cottage for two with distinctly Scandinavian accents. Covered with paint, the couple played Tom Sawyer and enlisted another friend to

From the sleeping loft one can look out the window at the river (above) or through the internal window at the activities in the living room (opposite).

Even a small cottage can find room for an interesting range of art and collections. By keeping to a narrow color palette, the combinations can cross many boundaries yet still manage to live in harmony.

help them, and all three went to work with enthusiasm and commendable perseverance.

For John and Tiff, the process was made much smoother when it accommodated his comfort level and allowed them a chance to test colors ahead of time. The walls are still white—although a softer, creamier white than the stark one he had started with. There is still plenty of wood, the furniture is still brown, and the new colors, though vivid, know their place. The color makeover did not displace his treasures, and the artwork looks wonderful on the newly painted walls. And it's definitely not too cute.

Because the house is so small, it was essential that the color choices share "equal" values—in this case, values based on the couple's personalities, collections, curtains, and pastimes. Tiff was able to allow her whimsical side to come out, and her husband-to-be was not displaced—only involved. "Small, normal elements of the house now stand out," observed John. "Ordinary doors have become special, and so have the views." And best of all—they're keeping the orange wall.

The stair balusters copy a traditional Swedish pattern. On the wall, John leads the pack in a black-and-white photograph from his speed-skating days.

PILLOWS

SUSAN SARGENT   Green Vines

RUG

PILLOWS

PILLOWS

BEDROOM PAINT

KITCHEN PAINT

LIVING ROOM PAINT

CURTAINS

RUG

SUSAN SARGENT   Black Desert Flowers

CHAPTER 6

the art of the country

"I want to wake up in the morning and be glad." That was how Barbara Van Vliet summed up her color-makeover expectations. The statement was simple but familiar: many people tell me how charmed they are when they see one of our color transformations. I knew that the project would be complex and gratifying.

Barbara is an artist herself—a watercolorist and graphic designer—and her color sense is highly evolved. What's more, she and her husband, Ben, knew that color represented the crowning touch to their eight-year effort to turn a weekend getaway into a permanent home that they could enjoy for the rest of their lives.

They're both refugees from the fast lane. For years the two of them pursued high-stress careers in a cosmopolitan community. Ben was a newspaperman whose talents took him from journalist to editor to publisher; Barbara owned an ad agency that grew from a one-woman

Shades of amber, yellow, tomato, orange, and currant unite the sitting room, where a rug is the focal point. Barbara repainted the armoire in tangerine.

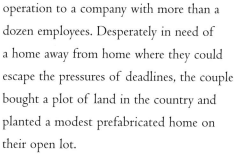

operation to a company with more than a dozen employees. Desperately in need of a home away from home where they could escape the pressures of deadlines, the couple bought a plot of land in the country and planted a modest prefabricated home on their open lot.

At first, they went there only on weekends. But within three years Ben and Barbara left the city behind and moved permanently into their country home. "It was a spiritual decision," recalled Barbara. "There was no real reason to stay where we were."

Barbara kept up with her career, taking on freelance clients and honing her artistic skills. She admits that it took a while for her to become accustomed to the slower pace of rural life, but as she relaxed within herself, she knew she'd made the right decision. "It was the best thing we ever did."

BRINGING THE INDOORS OUT: Hannah the dog checks out the model sailboat in the backyard pond. Bright weather-resistant fabrics spark up a family of wicker chairs.

feathering the nest

Barbara and Ben upgraded the basic interior of their prefab house, adding molding, hardwood floors, and other details. With its country vernacular and nice proportions, no one would ever guess it had been delivered to the site on two flatbed trucks.

The couple then masterminded an addition, practically doubling the size of the original structure, which gave them a living room that offered great light and views of their garden and pond.

Ben, now retired, turned his energies to landscaping. A passionate gardener since childhood, he graced the house and its surrounding acreage with magical borders, trellises, and outdoor settings.

the family of purple

BLUE PLUS RED EQUALS PURPLE. You probably learned this tidy fact in an introductory art class, maybe as far back as finger-painting time in elementary school. A jar of red, a jar of blue, a stick to mix them together—et voilà, purple. A fine start. But to me, *purple* can't begin to describe the variety of shades that result when red and blue get together.

Color professionals, who study both pigment and light, don't say "purple." They say "violet." Violet is the seventh and last color of the spectrum, and it represents noble spiritual aspiration—the highest quality a person can attain—according to chromopaths. In music, it is the color of B, the key in which much sacred music is written. Astronomers know it as the symbol of Jupiter; astrologists associate it with people born under the sign of Sagittarius; and voodoo practitioners consider it the color of power.

OTHER PURPLE FACTS

* It was Cleopatra's favorite color.
* As the rare and costly Tyrian purple, **obtained from shells in the Tyrian Sea, it was the color of royalty and cardinals' robes until the fall of Byzantium in 1453.**
* It is widow's garb in Thailand, **fasting and faith in the Ukraine.**
* Amethyst **is one of purple's most famous offspring. Healers have long used the semiprecious gem to quiet the mind and help curb addictive behaviors, especially alcoholism. Its reputation as a sobering influence is based in Greek myth. The story goes that Bacchus, god of wine, condemned Amethyst, an innocent young woman, to death. The goddess Diana was outraged and turned Amethyst into white crystal, thus rendering her immortal. Frustrated, Bacchus poured wine on the beautiful Amethyst, giving her—and the stone that bears her name—a purplish tint for eternity.**

* In traditional Japanese garb and ceremony, **the many varieties of** *murasaki* **(purple) are so important that they're given highly specific names.** *Kobai* is a plum-pink; *fuji* is the color of wisteria; *keshi murasaki* is a grayish purple; *ebi* is red-violet; *koki* is deep violet; and *usuki* is pale violet. **Each can represent subtle changes in the seasons. No matter what the month, however, the** *murasaki* **family is stately and royal.**

Women are often thought to have better color vision than men, and there is evidence to support that belief. We have more color receptors, on average, and there is much less color blindness among females. But some men can claim a finely tuned color sense, too. Barbara had what she describes as her epiphany, and knew the thing that was missing was to saturate their retirement home with color. Ben, with his gardener's eye, couldn't wait to see the colors of his beloved garden extend into the interior of his home. This step would complete their relocation adventure and give them the house they had dreamed of.

ABOVE: The gardening theme extends throughout the house, with art and textiles.

Ben's flower garden
reflects his love of color.

rugs: the maps of your world

REMEMBER IN THIRD GRADE, ON THE FIRST DAY OF SCHOOL, WHEN THE TEACHER WOULD REACH FOR A LITTLE TAB ABOVE THE BLACKBOARD AND PULL DOWN A MAP OF THE WORLD? There it was, all the continents and oceans laid out on a flat surface with four corners. The colors of those continents, countries, and oceans symbolized the beautiful lands that you'd visit in your mind for the rest of that brand-new school year.

In the home, rugs can also function as maps. A many-hued rug can serve as a key to the other colors in the home, pulling them all together so that they make sense. Rugs can be the key to our chosen palette, a guide to our personal geography of color.

Rugs have excited us for centuries and across cultures. The range is as vast as diverse continents, materials, and races can make them. But whether wool, silk, cotton, or manmade fibers, they share certain attributes.

First and most obviously, they are literally "floor coverings." From the dusty floors of yurts in the Himalayas to the frozen tundra in Lapland to the cold stone floors of European castles, rugs and carpets were one of the first home furnishings—easily portable, forgiving of hasty packing and rough use, both functional and decorative. Over the years, making higher forms of rugs (call them carpets)* became one of the most elaborate and

complex of the decorative arts. Fine hand-knotted carpets from Persia or India or China represent centuries of skills—many now almost lost because of machine-age production.

Today there are rugs for every style, taste, and budget, both new and antique. Rug choices are vast and can be overwhelming. Some common varieties are hooked rugs, tufted rugs, knotted rugs, flat-weave dhurries, fuzzy flokatis, shaggy ryas, indoor-outdoor, grass-fiber rugs, printed nylon, and the ubiquitous wall-to-wall in wool or synthetic fibers.

For anyone working to decorate his or her home, rugs offer a wealth of opportunity. Some people buy the rug first, falling for a color and design and then building their room around it. Others like the rug to be the pièce de résistance, the final flourish when everything else has been taken care of.

*A word about names: In the producing countries such as India, *rug* is not a good word—it means a cheap model, usually a simple flat weave, whereas a *carpet* is good quality and the real thing. In America absolutely everything for the floor is lumped together as a "floor covering"—including linoleum and engineered laminated wood. Wall-to-wall is always carpeting, but Orientals can be either rugs or carpets. In general, *rug* seems to be the name most generally used for any room rugs that are not wall-to-wall.

I am naturally biased in favor of handmade rugs, as I was trained to weave them, and have designed and imported them for my company for the past ten years. The ones I relate to are real design elements, not background music. What I love about rugs is that they are art for the floor. They're an opportunity to be creative and colorful in a place that is simply begging for attention.

An accent rug is less of a commitment than painting a room or a total reupholstering. You can move a rug around, trying it in different spaces and against different accessories. In many cases larger rug stores will let you take one home and try it out before making a decision.

True, it can be a challenge to work a vibrant rug into a staid decor with lots of traditional prints and dim coloring. Rug shopping can be a pivotal moment in the direction of your home.

If you are a victim of the sterile-neutral interior syndrome, a bright area or accent rug can be your quickest and most immediate fix to add color. A rug and a couple of bright pillows can totally change the mood and atmosphere and launch you on your own journey of discovery of how to expand your eye.

During our transformations, we used a lot of rugs. In some cases they were the starting point and were factored into the decisions that were

"Rugs...are art for the floor."

made at each step. Other times, the rug came later, as we experimented with different styles and colorings. Different designs and colors affect everything else around it, and we always knew when we had the right one. The whole world—at least the one under this roof—came together.

artist, inhibited

One would think that working artists would have a huge advantage when choosing colors for their homes. Don't they spend their work time making hundreds of color decisions every hour? Oddly enough, people who make good paintings or excel at graphic design don't necessarily shine when it comes to turning their dwellings into works of art.

Making a decision on a canvas or a computer screen—a decision that can be instantly eliminated—is a lot easier than committing to a color direction in a room. In art, colors are often built up in layers and are almost always read as part of a whole composition rather than judged as colors unto themselves. I've also observed that artists who work in two-dimensional formats are hyperaware of how colors will look in small doses on a flat plane but can be ill-equipped to visualize a single color on large walls in a three-dimensional space, or to imagine how fabrics will mix together on different pieces of furniture.

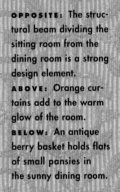

OPPOSITE: The structural beam dividing the sitting room from the dining room is a strong design element.
ABOVE: Orange curtains add to the warm glow of the room.
BELOW: An antique berry basket holds flats of small pansies in the sunny dining room.

artist, unleashed

Barbara used her artist's hand to paint the staircase (above) and the bedroom floor (opposite). The bedroom uses shades of pink found in the garden: geranium, fuchsia, and rose.

Barbara wasn't afraid of color, at least in theory. She knew she wanted a bedroom that felt like the tropics, a music room that made a statement, and a warm and cheerful dining room. She didn't need major therapy—just a little hand-holding while she worked her way through color ideas.

One of Barbara's decorating goals was to give each area a personality of its own. This wasn't going to be easy, considering that the first floor has an open floor plan, in which the great room bleeds into the dining room and kitchen, which in turn opens onto a small sitting room. She had always been particularly glum about this small area on the west end of the house, originally an awkward living room before the addition gave them a better space. It had never seemed to have any personality at all, despite a nice vintage hutch and a piano. The stairs took up one corner. The front door (never used) chopped up one wall, and the room had lost its identity. Was it an entry area, a small parlor, or simply a transit zone?

In the end, colors and fabrics were chosen for the downstairs that achieved all of Ben and Barbara's goals. Warm golds in the dining room, plaids and tomato red for the big living room, and sage and plum in the orphan room—now back in business as a room with attitude.

We helped Barbara with the walls, but she tackled the floors on her own. A quick study, she painted pale green and cream faux tiles on her bedroom floor—a project that took two solid weeks. She had ripped the original wall-to-wall off the stairs, wanting to create a carpet effect "without the carpet." Using her computer, and inspired by Albers's

In addition, artists must tremble slightly for their professional pride. It's one thing for old Sally Biggs to choose a poisonous green—after all, she is a banker and works with numbers all day, what would you expect? But it's quite another for a professional artist to expose to the world that she misjudged and chose—gasp—a color more like Pepto-Bismol than peony, or one more like a jar of mustard than a Tuscan villa.

color studies, she laid out a geometric stair runner in five colors taken from elements in the downstairs rooms. She then returned to the small sitting room, where the stairs began. She painted the hutch a new tangerine and added a geometric stencil of orange blocks on the single plum wall.

For the master bedroom, Barbara and Ben wanted a Bermuda feel, so they chose a coral and peach with raspberry and lime accents, perfect for that gentle climate. The bedding on the vintage brass bed was also coral, and they reupholstered a small green armchair to coordinate with the new diamond-patterned floor. Down the hall and into Ben's domain, his dressing room received a hearty dose of a color between gray and purple—think delphiniums or lupines, seen in a heavy fog.

Barbara and Ben have gotten what they wanted, and the house practically sings with its new colors. Barbara has also gotten a taste for the decorative work itself: when last heard from, she had done two rounds of sponging on the master-bedroom walls and had painted a grapevine around the kitchen doorway. All the colors work together to create a dreamily bright home for the artist and the gardener. A home for creativity, socializing, and relaxation. A home for life.

A delicate vine pattern on this periwinkle wallpaper turned a dull bathroom into a sanctuary.

working notes

DRESSING ROOM PAINT

PILLOWS

BEDROOM PAINT

CURTAINS

RUG

PILLOWS

PILLOWS

SUSAN SARGENT   Plum Floral

RUG YARN

MUSIC ROOM/STAIRS PAINT

a cozy home in the big city

An eclectic collection of handmade roosters is grouped on shelves in the pale green living room. The roomy eat-in kitchen is vibrant in yellow, red, and orange—colors inspired by a collection of pottery. On the dining-room wall is a silk screen depicting a Vermont landscape, and a vintage stitched sampler that reads "Houses should be lived in / Dogs should be on sofas." And there really is a dog. He's a Weimaraner named Tucker who indeed feels he owns the furniture.

Sounds like a house in the country, doesn't it?

Surprisingly, it's a duplex brownstone on the Upper West Side of Manhattan, about as far removed from the country as you can get.

Heidi Guldbrandsen, a thirty-one-year-old in finance, bought the place in the spring of 2003. "When I first saw the apartment it "had floor-to-ceiling mirrors, high-gloss white paint on every wall, and green shag carpeting," she recalled. That's a lot of paint and mirrors—the apartment has twelve-foot ceilings.

This petite urban living room proves that color can be essential in small spaces. Mixed fabrics and silhouettes create a welcoming shelter for city life.

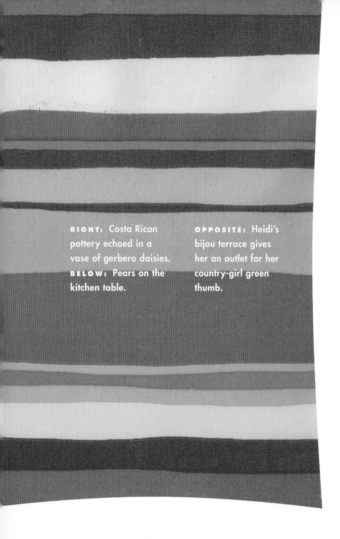

RIGHT: Costa Rican pottery echoed in a vase of gerbera daisies. **BELOW:** Pears on the kitchen table. **OPPOSITE:** Heidi's bijou terrace gives her an outlet for her country-girl green thumb.

Maximizing the glare was track lighting, which the previous owner had used to illuminate her art collection.

Typical of classic brownstone structures, the ground-floor apartment was narrow, with exposed brick walls that ran the length of both floors, from the front door to the back garden. And, of course, iron bars on the windows. An enviable location, but a bit too city for Heidi, who is a country girl at heart. She loves her life, her job, and her fabulous neighborhood, but she wanted to come home to a cozy space, a respite from the concrete canyons of the financial district where she works Monday to Friday. Having found her dream apartment, she sought to create a relaxing retreat in the middle of the city that would give her the ease and calming feeling of her beloved Vermont.

red ramble

RED IS THE "IT" COLOR, AND HAS BEEN SINCE PREHISTORIC TIMES. Cave paintings, totem poles, war paint, and Neolithic pottery were all tinted red with dyes mined from the earth or made from roots or insects. In primitive languages, red was often the only color that had its own word. (All others were known as "light" or "dark.")

- Across cultures and centuries, red has been a sacred color. Mayan high priests wore red robes. The pope wears red slippers, and red signifies fire, sacrifice, and charity in the Catholic Church. In ancient Hebrew, the name of Adam—the first man, according to the Old Testament—means both "red" and "alive."

- It has also signaled violence, rage, blood, and war. Mars, both the planet and the god of war, is always associated with the color red. It stands for passion, vigor, and courage in voodoo, and red was the marching color for revolutionary Russia.

- Healers and spiritualists associate red with energy and health. For chromopaths, red is used to stimulate circulation and to treat depression and anemia. It is prescribed for apathy and for "those cursed with a repugnance for humanity."

- Our "red letter day" comes from a fifteenth-century practice of marking calendars with red symbols to indicate holy days.

- Red is a power color in our society; powerful women wear red suits, power ties are often red, and red muscle cars have a presence unlike any other.

- In China, red is the color of luck and plays an important role at weddings, New Year's Eve celebrations, and other observances and rituals.

- Red is the color of love, and we use the symbolism of red hearts and red roses.

- Red is believed to have healing properties. Edward II's physician tried to ward off smallpox by surrounding the king with red; two hundred years later, Francis I was wrapped in a scarlet blanket to protect him from disease. In Ireland and Russia, red flannel was believed to prevent scarlet fever; in Scotland it was used to relieve sprains; in Portugal red coral was a headache remedy. In colonial Massachusetts, any family with a medical emergency would raise a red flag outside to call for a doctor. And today all over the world a red cross or a red crescent symbolizes medical relief and the life-giving infusion of blood.

- Red is also about danger, passion, and damnation. The devil is red, as are the fires of hell. Dangerous women are scarlet, and vamps have hot red lipstick and very high-heeled shoes. Stop signs are red and alert us to danger ahead. In motorcycle racing, to "redline" means to accelerate beyond a tachometer's safety zone.

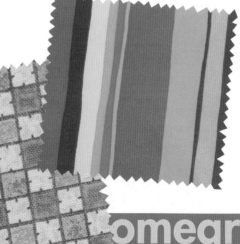

Yeats once wrote that "red is the color of magic in every country." In home decorating, red is a popular choice to work its magic in endless variations. Somewhere between love, luck, and hell there are reds that excite us and compel us and that are wonderful for furnishings. Above all, red is warm, nurturing, comforting, and available in shades from the hottest crimsons to the slinkiest fuchsias to the spiciest tomatoes.

Roman shades in a flowery pattern screen Heidi's kitchen from the street outside. The tall cupboards are lacquered red.

country vs. kountry

When it comes to interior design, "country" decor has gotten a bad rap. Too many people associate country with wimpy pastels, cutesy wallpaper, and geese with bows. But what they think of as country is actually a kitschy style mutation one might call "country with a *k*," i.e., kountry.

What's the difference between country and kountry? For one thing, kountry is fake. It's marked by such inauthentic "artifacts" as miniature straw hats crowned with polyester flowers, faux antique signs advertising seed packets, and finishes that have been artificially aged. Walk into any Cracker Barrel restaurant and you'll see what I mean—kountry kute is

The pale lime walls of the dining room reflect the cool backyard and show-case a vintage—and appropriate—embroidery.

all over the place, celebrating (and selling) a
warm and fuzzy version of history that's been
given the full Disney treatment, via Norman
Rockwell.

Heidi, thankfully, is country with a *c.*
She's a devotee of that wild woman we call
Mother Nature, who uses colors with a bold,
imaginative, and uninhibited hand. In real
country interiors, we don't mess with Mother
Nature. Reds can be as vibrant as tulips in the
spring; yellows are allowed to be as bright as
marigolds; greens recall lush fields or the ten-
der stalks of new plants; blues are every shade
ever known in a summer sky. With nature as a
muse, the door is opened to vivid colors and
patterns that play off one another's strengths,
resulting in a space that is warm, comfortable,
and invigorating, like the countryside itself.

Country style is by no means restricted
to rural zip codes, however. It can be hip and
witty when it needs to be, as long as it takes a
wide detour around anything cute, twee, overly
folksy, or contrived. It might offer pride of
place to countrified archetypes—such as a
collection of folk roosters—yet can present
these icons with humor and taste, making
them work within the context of young, cool
urban life.

from high gloss to high style

Heidi's first goal as a Manhattan homeowner
was to get rid of the track lighting and the
gloss paint. She made arrangements to jettison
her dark, heavy leather furniture, which was too
big for the ninety-two-inch-wide living room,
and just plain wrong for the space. As a woman
who knew what she didn't want, it was easy
for Heidi to make subtractions. That mission

OPPOSITE: Tall storage cabinets echo the colors of a favorite pottery collection. Beyond, a hall leads to the dining room and out to the tiny back garden.

ABOVE: Heidi's pottery collection inspired her creative kitchen.

accomplished, she was at a standstill with a barely furnished apartment. She had to entertain for business and was tired of having people walk in and say, "Oh! You just moved in?"

Heidi needed a little help furnishing and beautifying her urban digs, but she didn't want a high-powered interior designer. She knew all about Manhattan makeovers, having seen the homes of several of her business partners undergo complete overhauls that were wildly disruptive, diabolically expensive, and excruciatingly trendy. She hated fussy chintz yet dreaded the prevailing fashion—a sort of retro-moderne minimalism. She didn't have the time or energy to battle the biases of a professional style snob.

We worked with Heidi on her makeover because she liked our comfortable approach.

"I didn't want anything to be too fancy," Heidi explained. "I wanted the whole place to be durable, and dog-friendly." She might also have added that she didn't feel a need to impress anybody and knew that a sophisticated version of country ease could work, even in the big city.

turning up the heat

An adventurous and athletic thirty-something, Heidi spends her free time traveling and on several trips to Costa Rica has collected handmade pottery. Each piece is a fabulous example of country color, brushed on with exuberance and a joyous lack of inhibition.

Studying her collection—"some of my favorite stuff in the entire world," she calls it—we helped her create a palette for her kitchen that included marigold yellow, fire engine red (for the tall cabinets), and rich orange (for cabinets over the stove and under the counters). For the inside of the open shelves that housed the pottery collection itself, we alternated swaths of violet and lavender that matched the patterns.

Five strong colors for one city kitchen may seem like a lot. But the kitchen, large for an apartment this size, has tall ceilings and floor-to-ceiling storage on both sides. It had previously been painted antiseptic gloss white with mirror insets, and Heidi's eye wanted

Several shades of pale green on the sequence of walls give an illusion of more space. Painting the duct yellow gives it an uncommon distinction and frames Tucker at his dinner.

living with brick

EXPOSED BRICK WALLS CAN BE A BLESSING. In otherwise featureless houses and apartments—places where Sheetrock is usually king—an expanse of natural brick can add soulfulness, a sense of history, an earthy note of authenticity. Bricks can be a handicap, too. Whether they cover an entire wall or merely surround a fireplace, they are usually a permanent design element whose color and texture must be reckoned with.

Are bricks your best friend, or your biggest challenge? It all depends on how you choose to handle them.

I have never had to deal with an overdose of brick in my own house. Our living-room fireplace is built of natural stone, while another building that I once reworked had lovely old brick outside, plastered and papered walls within. But in the course of creating the interiors for this book, there were two very different locations where brick had to be dealt with: one was Heidi's narrow urban apartment, with brick on all four sides. The other was Stephanie and Stan's home, a traditional Cape with a prominent brick fireplace wall. In both cases we found the brick to be a problem, which needed to be solved.

BRICK TIPS

* I appreciate the look of aged natural bricks, yet given my love of color, a little goes a long way. Natural brick encompasses a whole range of tones, which may include terra-cotta, burnt umber, sienna, pink, or liver-colored tones. It's virtually impossible to find a paint or fabric that "matches" brick. What might be satisfying in one medium can make you wince in another. Bricks are made of earth, so one common option is to take a cue from the earth-tone palette with related shades—soft red browns, warm chocolates, and terra-cotta. Good accent colors for natural brick can be warm yellows, creams, golds, and olives.

* Another option is to paint right over those bricks. In Heidi's New York apartment, we compromised, leaving some walls of the original brick untouched but painting three walls of the living room. With only one window at the back end, we wanted to lighten the feel and downplay the darkness. Stan and Stephanie (see chapter 3) didn't realize how much they loathed their smoky brick fireplace until we painted their living room burnt orange instead of the dreary brown it had been before. We whitewashed the brick gently, which took the edge off the color and put it in friendly harmony with the glowing walls.

* However nice the brick, sometimes it just doesn't jibe with our decorating goals. Still, we don't have to let it tie our hands. Brick offers plenty of opportunities for creativity. On a structural wall, you could dry-brush every fifth brick with your favorite color or paint the whole thing in alternating colors like a giant textile. You could tint the mortar black, train pots of English ivy or morning glories, adorn it with antique toasting forks, cover it with a collection of decorative china, or chalk each brick with ancient runes. Paneling or woodwork can be installed to cover it up, or it could simply get disguised with a coat of paint to neutralize it and make it recede, out of your sight.

* If you have a large fireplace that reads as a light-sucking black hole in the off-season, various types of fire screens, flowers, or props can fill that yawning opening. In wrought iron, découpaged or stenciled wood, crewelwork, or painted

freehand swirls, fire screens have been around forever, and creating your own is a rewarding activity.

◆ Think of your fireplace as a display wall, even though it's closer to the floor than to the ceiling. Use it to show off favorite objects, preferably ones too big for a bookshelf, or fill the opening with little white lights or candles. My grandfather, born in 1889, used to swear by stiff, folded fans of gold paper leaning back against the andirons. Whatever your choice, don't let your brick defeat or intimidate you.

all together, now

Envision the living/dining room area of this vintage brownstone. Both sides of the ground floor are long, windowless brick walls. The wall on the right side of the living room had been painted a frightening high-gloss white by the previous owner, shifting into exposed and sooty brick around the fireplace. On the opposite wall, where the dining table was placed, the brick was exposed. Heidi wanted the gloss gone, so we overpainted with a very pale green. On the dining-room side, we left the brick natural, which works well with a dark wood table that seats twelve, Windsor-style dining chairs, and a large and heavy carved French armoire. Typical of this kind of space, where a brownstone has been chopped into apartments, there are lots of little walls, angles, closets in odd places, and tiny halls. We used four different variations of the same yellow-green for fun, and to give a sense of dimension. We defined the elements of the staircase wall with a bolder green, an orange door, and a yellow duct.

New furniture in the living room was of moderate size, upholstered in fabrics that incorporated sage, warm paprika, and burnt orange. Bold geometric window treatments and colorful rugs underscored the sophisticated country feel.

Upstairs, two bedrooms—small but with high ceilings—were made over in a mix of Heidi's favorite colors, including lavender, teal, gray-green, and periwinkle, with funky, bright bedding in hot pink in the guest bedroom, and a blue-and-teal paisley fabric on her own bed.

"It's all tied together," she said of her unabashed interior. "The paints, trim, borders, furniture . . . when you walk from the kitchen

ABOVE AND OPPOSITE:
Tall ceilings can become less intimidating by adding a decorative border and vertical stripes. In this narrow bedroom, what might have been cell-like is instead a cozy nest with hot pink bedding.

relief and immediate, major change. "A few degrees one way or the other, and they could have looked like kids' colors, or circus colors," said Heidi. "But the assortment came out right and added warmth and depth. While the makeover was going on, every day I'd come home from work and see something new."

"The look is modern,
but it doesn't feel contrived."

through the living room, into the backyard, it all makes sense. The look is modern, but it doesn't feel contrived—it feels natural and fluid."

After all was decorated and done, Heidi has indeed enjoyed showing off her new domain to friends, family, and business colleagues. "People who saw the place when I first bought it don't even recognize it now," said Heidi. But she recognizes it. To her, it looks like home.

OPPOSITE: In the master bedroom, two-layered curtains block the city out and coordinate with the bedding—all in Heidi's favorite teals and blues. **BELOW:** Small details such as the doorknobs painted in teal refer back to the accent colors in the fabrics.

working notes

HALL/DOOR PAINT

KITCHEN PAINT

RUG

dots are cream on brown

dots are lighter green on dark green

OTTOMAN

SUSAN SARGENT

Checkmate Green

CHAIR

LIVING ROOM
PAINT

RUG

COFFEE TABLE

CHAIR

SUSAN
SARGENT

Dot Grid
Green

GUEST ROOM
PAINT

MASTER
BEDROOM
PAINT

COUCH

CURTAINS

CHAPTER 8

a cinderella story

The pages of shelter magazines tend to showcase fine old homes with high ceilings and classical trim and woodwork. They also devote many pages to modern masterpieces with two-story fireplaces and dramatic glass walls, anonymous trophy houses with million-dollar decorating, lofts that look like operating rooms, and other excesses of the rich and trendy. You might read an occasional feature about novelty homes that are, say, converted fishing shacks or former coal sheds or eccentric pavilions made out of recycled bottles.

But what you don't often see in glossy publications are simple, affordable homes in contractor-built subdivisions. These places fly below the radar of most high-style, show-off magazines. Yet with serious doses of color, even a basic, modest house can become interesting and original, transformed without great expense into a home with personality and charm.

Generic denim sofas get a hot date in a living room done in plum and lime.

INSPIRATION

ABOVE: The spirit of this lively house for a young family is expressed in nature's colors.

RIGHT: In the children's playroom, table and chairs were painted in bright stripes to coordinate with a lighthearted chandelier.
OPPOSITE: One thing leads to another: once the piano was painted in cheery shades, the plain walls called for freehand painting.

Karin and Andy Nicholson can attest to that. They'd been living in their "starter home" for nearly five years. For most of that time they rented the house and thus were forced to live with relentlessly white walls. The situation was aesthetically painful for the couple, because both of them are crazy about color— and so are their two young children.

"Everything was *so* plain," recalled Karin. They did their best to liven up their home with playful pieces, including a hand-painted hutch in the dining area, a pair of blue sofas in the living room, Matisse posters, and a multicolored "chandelier" that's as festive as a jester's hat. But the whiteness was overwhelming and actually made these colorful

pieces seem out of place, as if they were just visiting for a spell and would go back to their "real" homes soon.

When Karin and Andy finally became owners, they were eager for a massive color transformation. Yet, though they painted the furniture in their daughter's bedroom a fetching periwinkle blue, they found themselves stricken with a kind of decorating paralysis when it came to choosing colors for their downstairs walls. "We wanted color, but we just didn't know how to get it up there," Karin explained.

It's not an uncommon syndrome.

Shopping for paint can be daunting, especially for first-timers. There's a dizzying array of options to be considered: not only colors, of which there are thousands, but also brands and finishes (i.e., flat, eggshell, satin, semigloss, and high gloss). Even after you've narrowed down your choices and decided that you want, say, a red living room in a semigloss finish, you'll no doubt find yourself with an overload of paint chip samples, studying them until

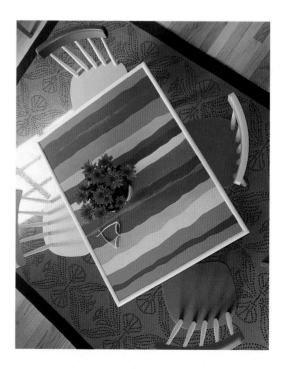

your eyes hurt. Will the Blaze or the Sunset Skyline look best? Is Porcelain Red too bright? What about Fire & Ice, Ruby Lips, Red Wine? This is the point at which many turn back, sigh mournfully, and settle for off-white after all. It's just too hard to make a decision.

might as well jump

When I took on the couple's project, we met at my studio to look at colors and fabrics, and to discuss ideas. Unlike less decisive people, Karin knew exactly where she wanted to head—and it was straight into the jaws of fuchsia, red, marigold, lime green, and plum. This was a young, energetic family, unafraid of taking risks. All they lacked was experience, and they were about to get some.

Andy, too, is intrepid. He spends his days managing a sales force for a local phone company. When he gets home, he wants to be with his family in a space where he can relax, frolic with the kids, and recharge. There was persuasive evidence that he had already been bitten by the color bug. A simple hutch he had made for their kitchen he painted eggplant. Its jaunty clock-tower roof had been painted hot-pepper orange.

OPPOSITE: Andy painted the corner hutch. The table is set, awaiting the arrival of Hannah's birthday party guests. **ABOVE:** A reproduction wall clock in retro orange.

can color make a room look smaller?

CHROMOPHOBES ASK ME THIS QUESTION ALL THE TIME. They believe that potent colors on their walls will visually shrink a space.

I tell them they're absolutely right, to a point. Certain colors—especially those that are deep, vibrant, or highly saturated—can emphasize the perimeters of a room, and thus seem to draw walls closer together.

There's a more important question, however, that nobody ever asks: Why does it matter?

Contrary to popular belief, bigger isn't automatically better. In fact, bigness is often the enemy of a happy home.

Example: I recently visited a friend who spent a fortune buying a dream house for his family of five. It was a massive McMansion with a soaring three-story foyer, a living room the size of a high school gym, a professional kitchen with every gourmet appliance known to man, and a dining room that could seat twenty. The whole place was oversize, and every wall and ceiling was painted white.

The family looked tiny in their enormous new house. My friend, his wife, and their three children were like ants, constantly scurrying for cover. All five of them avoided the cavernous living room and dining room, huddling instead in a smallish den in the back of the house, where they were comforted by the TV, the stereo, the telephone, and a wall of books. I suspect it was the only room on the ground floor that didn't echo.

That McMansion was desperate for color. It needed to become warm and personal; those walls were begging to be reclaimed, to be brought down to earth with colors that wrapped themselves around the family the house was built to shelter. And if it did indeed make the rooms look smaller—the family might reclaim the house they now found so overwhelming.

Basic white cabinets and a standard floor plan do not mean a kitchen has to be dull. A combination of accent colors on doors, walls, and trim makes plain details sparkle.

room size Rx

THERE ISN'T A SINGLE COLOR IN THE WHOLE WIDE WORLD THAT WILL ACTUALLY CHANGE THE SQUARE FOOTAGE OF A ROOM. But whether your space is large or small, colors can have a profound impact on its perceived size.

◆ Deep, saturated colors such as beet red, raspberry, blueberry, ripe plum, and Concord grape can make a big, ungainly room seem cozy and can enhance a small space by turning it into an intimate jewel box of a room. Such colors have the power to create a womb with a view—a space that people are automatically drawn to and which makes them feel safe, protected, and comfortable.

◆ Mild blues (cornflower, periwinkle, sky); serene violets (hydrangea, lavender, heather); bluish greens (teal, aqua, turquoise); and millions of other cool hues are known as "receding" colors. If you've ever taken an art class, you already

know that these colors are excellent for backgrounds of landscapes and still lifes, because they seem to hover in the distance. In the home, various blues and blue-based shades visually smudge the corners of a room; when ceilings are painted to match, the surfaces can seem to dissolve into the stratosphere. It's unlikely that such colors will actually make a room look larger, but they can add an atmospheric quality that makes a person forget size and remember beauty.

◆ Hot, lively colors such as grapefruit yellow and tangerine orange produce visual vibrations and give walls a presence that can't be ignored. When streaming sunlight bounces off yellow/orange walls, the room glows, as if surrounded by a ring of fire. At night, those walls dance in the artificial light of whatever fixture is turned on. There's nothing small about these hot colors. And although they may not visually grow or shrink a room, they create excitement and set the stage for human activity.

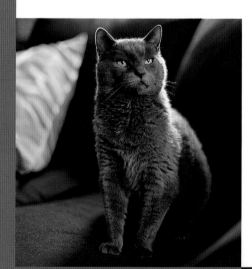

In the daytime, the modest-size living room is filled with sun, and its plum and green is much appreciated by the cat.

BELOW: What to do with an uninspiring hall? Alternating colors on the trim and doors fill it with energy suitable for young children's games. A do-it-yourself section of wainscoting is painted bright green and matches a decorative wallpaper and border.

OPPOSITE: Stools in mixed, non-matching colors are a quick way to personalize a kitchen counter.

RIGHT: Colorful candles are always an easy color accent.

hall, while around it are four main rooms and a powder room, opening onto one another: living room, playroom, eat-in kitchen, powder room, study. The living room and playroom have wooden floors, but the rest of the ground floor is a sea of gray slate tiles—durable but a challenging color to work with. The kitchen cabinets were classic white ready-mades.

We laid out a plan using Karin's color choices as a starting point, focusing on a piece of bold striped fabric called Barefoot, in her selected colors. (This fabric would later be interpreted in paint on the children's table and chairs.) Karin was busy with her two small children, and they moved in with a neighbor for a few days while the painting was going on. Andy had offered to take a week off and give us a hand. (In the end, it was actually we who gave *him* a hand. He got right into the spirit of things.) Although Andy hadn't done much painting before, he was eager to try and recruited two of his buddies (also non-painters) to assist. A day off with a good stack of CDs, many pots of coffee, and a can of Habanero-Pepper paint—it doesn't get much better than this.

As philosopher Horace once noted, "He who has begun has half done." Once they were in gear, the painting proceeded quickly. Monitoring the progress was like opening a present each day, and the couple surprised us as well with their own great ideas. It was Karin who suggested we paint the kids' piano—a functional but not valuable upright. She and Andy were up for anything, and their enthusiasm was infectious and exhilarating. Soon we could hardly keep up with them—parents and children were becoming confident and empowered to take on their new colorful world.

ABOVE: Transition zone. The home office across the hall from the living room ties back in by echoing the kiwi green used on the wainscoting. **OPPOSITE:** The same plum and green story continues across the hall by the front door, using a plum wool runner to connect the zones.

On the kitchen wall was a matching orange reproduction clock, and the family's dishes and table linens were also lively and bright. All they needed was a little help to release their inner color and give it a bigger stage.

Like most starter homes, the house has a simple floor plan. If you imagine a squared-off doughnut, the center is the staircase and

"He who has begun
has half done."
—HORACE

kids and color

KARIN AND ANDY'S LITTLE BOY, JAKE, LIES IN BED AND NAMES THE COLORS of the sailboats that float along, at eye level, on the border of his bedroom wallpaper. Babies recognize colors before they recognize shapes. "Color names were some of Jake's first words," said his father, Andy.

If you think that kids are in love only with primary colors or can name only the basic colors of the rainbow—red, yellow, orange, green, blue, or purple—then you're underestimating their powers of color perception.

Color expert Ro Logrippo, who designs spaces for children, polled five hundred kids in five different countries to find out what they liked best about their rooms. She asked them to write down the color of their bedroom in

their own words. To her surprise, she received twenty-six different color descriptions, including "turquoise," "mauve," and "Manhattan beige."

Beige probably isn't the best choice for kids. Most children crave actively colored rooms; psychologists say it's because the vibrancy matches the child's own energy level and holds his or her attention. Researchers have found that warm colors and brilliant lighting in the classroom cause a measurable increase in children's brain activity.

But that doesn't mean kids need obvious palettes. They're more sophisticated than we think, and instead of offering them commercially selected "juvenile primaries," we should be allowing them to please themselves with their natural (and adventurous) color choices. Those of us who have become more timid over the years and have forgotten the joys of a really big crayon box might do well to expand our color horizons by getting in tune with the open-mindedness of children.

CLOCKWISE FROM UPPER LEFT: Jake enjoys the colors of his new bedroom. Guests Wally and Florrie make use of the playroom. Hannah (center left) and friends attend to the gaily colored cake.

kid spaces, grown-up spaces, family rooms

Today, Karin and Andy's kitchen is a cheerful place with harvest moon walls, a ceiling beam the color of red peppers, and multicolored doors. The dining table is lighthearted enough to host a kid's birthday party, yet sophisticated enough for a sit-down dinner after the little ones have gone to bed. The cabinets are still white, but the room has the enfolding warmth of hearth and home.

The living room was a different story. Parents of young children need to set aside their own spaces, too, so this room was designed strictly for grown-ups. The color palette was plum, grass green, and blue, and we worked around the pair of blue denim sofas the couple had purchased not long before. Lined draperies and structured valances in lustrous green maintain a sense of humor via

frisky trim. The walls, painted a rich plum color, put on a show as the light moves around the house during the day and into the evening. A contemporary geometric rug picks up the plum of the walls, the green of the curtains, and the denim color of the sofas. "It's so swanky," said Karin of the living room. "We feel like we're in a jazz club."

Directly next door—between the husky-voiced living room and the family-friendly kitchen—is a space dedicated to the children. It's a place for puzzles, music, make-believe, and tea parties, with a bright green upright piano and a miniature table and chairs painted in hot stripes. Its walls remain white—a choice so basic that Karin and Andy, long snow-blinded by their interior, initially balked at it. But in the interest of providing a resting place for the eyes, maximizing natural light, and separating the marmalade dining/cooking areas from the

The master bedroom (opposite) is done in a red paisley theme, using fuchsia and blue as counterpoints. The wallpaper border echoes the fabric, as do the turnover tops (above) of the curtains.

fire. A balanced decorating scheme applies not only to color, form, and flow—it also ensures that both adults and children have spaces to call their own, as well as spaces to share.

Our last step was bringing to life the long hall running the length of the house. At one end is the tail of the living room's plum wall. At the other, the kitchen. In between, doors to the powder room and study break the south wall, and the staircase, with a half wall instead of a railing, rises in the center. This space was an irresistible opportunity for some color magic.

The lovely thing about halls is that they are transit zones. You can take more chances there than you might in a room where you spend a lot of time. For Karin and Andy's hall, we determined to give it real personality. Wainscoting—the affordable kind that comes in four-foot lengths and can be installed in an hour—looks just like the real thing when it's painted spring green and gets a little strip of molding on top. We wallpapered the upper walls and put up a border along the top. The door casings we painted in lilac (study) and fuchsia (powder room). The front door we painted a deep, rich blueberry. A couple of bright runners divide the slate floor, and the hall is now the crown jewel of the house.

happy endings

Not for one minute did Karin and Andy worry about having an orange kitchen, a green and yellow playroom, a plum living room, or a wallpapered hallway that's half green/half patterned with many-hued trim. Quite the opposite. "This is really our taste," said Karin. Andy went one step further: "This is like winning the lottery," he said.

ABOVE: Hannah chose stripes and flowers in her favorite colors of pale lilac and soft green. **OPPOSITE:** Jake's bedroom was decorated with a sailboat theme, using coordinated bedding and wallpaper.

plum living room, I urged the couple to allow the room to stay neutral. In the end, I had fun painting freehand "trees" that crawl up the walls with swirly branches in yellow and green in a satisfying Seussian manner.

Though the transformed living room opens right onto the playroom, there's no mistaking which room is for board books and juice boxes and which is for late-night tête-à-têtes by the

working notes

LIVING ROOM PAINT

KITCHEN PAINT

CURTAIN BORDER

CURTAINS

HALL PAINT

DEN/UPSTAIRS PAINT

RUG

RUG

SUSAN SARGENT *Willow Plum*

SUSAN SARGENT *Bamboo*

the white apartment

In Asian cookery there is a dish called congee. Basically a gruel of rice and water, it's as white as new-fallen snow and tastes as bland as baby food. Nobody eats it plain, however (except babies). What people do is use it as a base for a startling variety of foods. I've eaten congee with curry, shrimp, vegetables, and even 100-year-old egg, and every time it's tasted entirely different.

If you're one of the millions of people who can't paint their walls because of cranky landlords, skeptical families, or any other reason, there are lots of other ways to bring color into your environment. Just think of your walls as congee, and yourself a master chef. You'll be amazed at how spicy you can make things.

I recently gave a color makeover to Astrid Viglund's all-white apartment, a challenge that allowed me some of my usual tools but took away options such as painting or wallpapering. As with so many rental spaces, the white wall

INSTANT COLOR: This all-white living room got colorful accessories in a one-day makeover. A bright rug, some painted wicker, and lots of cushions add spice to the plain vanilla.

The "before" living room (above) was a pale environment. The old-fashioned kitchen sink had a neutral skirt (below) before it emerged in a new lime outfit (opposite).

color couldn't be changed. But this particular place was whiter than usual, because the apartment's tenant, owner of a funky retail store downtown, collected antique linens and ceramics and was enamored with white.

It's a nice Zen-like look, and we decided to show both before and after views of the apartment. In the "before" shots, there is not a drop of color anywhere, except the natural pine of some vintage pieces. In the "after" photos, you see how we accented with ceramics, rugs, pillows, a couple of bright wicker chairs for an instant change of mood.

Despite my color fetish, I have to admit that I like the white version, too. Most probably, somewhere in between the two extremes lies a comfort zone for most of us.

We worked from a palette of pink, green, fuchsia, and orange for the living room, retaining the white linen sofa and chairs. We painted a bookshelf to display a collection of bright Japanese pottery that belonged to the owner but that was usually kept, inexplicably, stored in a closet. For the two bedrooms, we did one in earth tones of gold, olive, and paprika, and the other in violet and plum.

Without changing the white walls, the home got to be Color Queen for a Day with a collection of new accessories and accents. The all-white walls provided an effective backdrop for an exciting collection of colors. Congee, it turns out, made an ideal base for a spicy dish of an apartment.

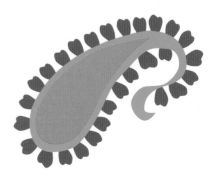

◆ Rugs can make an enormous difference and enliven even the blandest room. **Find an accent rug you love and use its palette as the jumping-off point for upholstery and other details.**

◆ Paint your furniture. **In the white apartment, we painted a pair of wicker chairs lime green and added hot pink cushions. They became a focus of the room and looked great against the white walls. Paint can be salvation for uninspired or bargain-priced dressers, bookcases, coffee tables, chests, and armoires . . . and don't** be afraid to further personalize your furnishings with a bit of freehand decorative painting.

◆ Play with fabric. **It's easy, and inexpensive, to add color interest through throw pillows, tablecloths, and curtains. In the white apartment, a skirt gathered under the edge of the sink counter added another color touch to the kitchen.**

◆ Hang bold artwork on your walls. **Don't limit yourself to paintings, posters, or prints; try masks, textiles, plates, vintage purses, flags, wreaths, decorative tiles, sheets of handmade paper, children's drawings, mirrors with painted frames, or whatever excites your eye and your sense of color.**

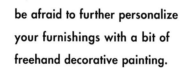

BEFORE AND AFTER ADDING SPICES: The original bedroom (right) was reimagined in earth tones (above).

LEFT AND BELOW: See how easily a simple substitution of colorful ceramics changed the impact of the kitchen corner.

You've Got the Power

As a color crusader, I'm often sought out for advice—by big businesses as well as humble apartment dwellers. During my conversations with the color-hungry, I am repeatedly asked if I aim to be the next design doyenne. I'm sure it's meant as a compliment, but my philosophies and practices are diametrically opposed to the purism, perfectionism, and labor-intensiveness of the M-woman's.

My style is more like Julia Child's. (In fact, I want to grow up to *be* Julia Child.) Home design, like gourmet cooking, tends to be way too serious. I don't believe most people really want a sterile, bland, perfect house any more than most of us want to achieve excruciatingly perfect meals. My core advice on color resembles Julia's on cooking: Try it! Splash it around! Spill it on the floor! Use more spices! Get messy! Have fun! And most of all, laugh while you're doing it. (I'm working on the voice.)

I have no doubt that one of the most important parts of our interactive makeover process was simply being there to get our homeowners started. I would be very surprised if

they don't take on more and more creative projects each year. We can't be there for everyone, but we can encourage and empower you to grab your brush and paint to enhance your skills, widen your eyes, and express your vision. Give yourself permission to make mistakes and, above all, enjoy the process.

"Our deepest fear is not that we are inadequate. Our deepest fear is that we are powerful beyond measure." So said Nelson Mandela in his 1994 presidential inaugural speech. "It is our light, not our darkness," he added, "that most frightens us." Though Mandela wasn't talking about color— at least, not the kind that comes in

cans—his message is clear: we shall be our best when we are our strongest, brightest selves.

Color can help, even transform. It is a powerful form of self-expression. In our visual vocabulary there are 7 million different colors, and each has a meaning that belongs to us alone. When we use them creatively, colors are gifts of light and liquid that are no less than magical.

"Your playing small doesn't serve the world," continued Mandela. "As we let our own light shine, we unconsciously give other people permission to do the same."

Mandela is a hero in a world with far more serious concerns than home design. But in our homes, we can nurture our families and ourselves, build our creativity and intellect, and prepare ourselves for the world and the challenges outside our doors.

The world is your palette. Be brave. Be yourself. Choose your colors, and let them glow.

source list/directory

Rugs, bedding, pillows, furniture, lamps, dinnerware, fabrics, trims, wallpaper, paints, decorative accessories, and interior design services available through:

Susan Sargent
132 Newbury Street
Boston, MA 02116
617-262-2226
Web site: www.susansargent.com

Susan Sargent
4783 Main Street
Manchester Center, VT 05255
800-245-4767 or 802-366-4955

paint source for susan sargent colors

Fine Paints of Europe
PO Box 419
Woodstock, VT 05759
800-332-1556
www.finepaints.com and at
www.susansargent.com

licensee contacts for susan sargent products

Robert Allen @ Home (fabrics)
55 Cabot Boulevard
Mansfield, MA 02048
800-333-3777
www.robertallendesign.com

Lexington Home Brands Furniture (furniture)
PO Box 1008
Lexington, NC 27293
800-LEX-INFO
www.lexington.com

Present Tense, Inc. (ceramics)
PO Box 1358
Sterling, VA 20167
800-282-7117
www.presenttense.com

York Wall (wallcoverings)
Available through
www.susansargent.com

Oriental Accent, Inc.
(decorative accessories)
13405 N. Stemmons Freeway
Farmers Branch, TX 75234
800-951-9005
www.orientalaccent.us

Mohawk Home
(pillows and printed rugs)
PO Box 12069
Calhoun, GA 30703
www.mohawkind.com

Noritake Dinnerware (dinnerware)
15–22 Fairlawn Avenue
Fair Lawn, NJ 07410
www.noritake.com

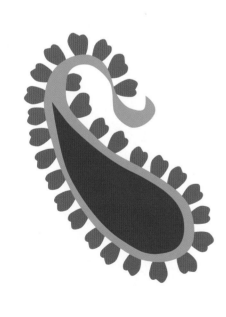

other sources

furniture

Maine Cottage Company Store
PO Box 935
Yarmouth, ME 04096
207-846-1430
www.mainecottage.com

Dan Mosheim
Dorset Custom Furniture
23 Goodwood Lane
Dorset, VT 05251
802-867-5541
www.dorsetcustomfurniture.com

Brown Jordan Company
9860 Gidley Street
El Monte, CA 91731
626-443-8971
www.brownjordan.com

bedding

Soko Company
44-02 Eleventh Street, Suite 503
Long Island City, NY 11101
718-392-5252
www.soko@kokocompany.com

Davenport Home Furnishings
MB & Company
19985 Oxnard Street
Woodland Hills, CA 91367
818-992-8965
www.davenporthomefurnishings.com

Hue
99 Hanover Street
Portland, ME 04101
207-772-4564
www.shophue.com

window treatments

Wendy Galbraith
353 Carlen Street
Manchester Center, VT 05255
802-362-7018

lamps

Simon Pearce
The Mill
Queechee, VT 05059
877-452-7763
www.simonpearce.com

Altamira
79 Joyce Street
Warren, RI 02885
401-245-7676
www.altamiralighting.com

Janna Ugone Lamps
1 Cottage Street
East Hampton, MA 01027
413-527-5530

lampshades

Lakes Lampshades
Pawlet, VT 05761
802-325-6309
www.lakeslampshades.com

decorative accessories

Stray Dog Imports
565 McFarland Avenue
Rossville, GA 30741
866-478-7297
www.straydogimports.com

wall art

Wild Apple Graphics
526 Woodstock Road
Woodstock, VT 05091
800-756-8359
www.wildapple.com

Suk Shuglie
1320-B Manheim Pike
Lancaster, PA 17601
717-393-0966
www.sukshuglie.com

Pamela Marron
802-867-2246
Horst Rodies
802-375-9067
Max Cooper
401-578-0349

antiques

Judy Pascal Antiques
PO Box 106
145 Elm Street
Manchester Center, VT 05255
802-362-2004
www.judypascal.com

decorative cakes

Mary Bandereck
Topsfield, MA 01983
978-887-7404

bibliography

Alexander, C., et al. *A Pattern Language.* New York: Oxford University Press, 1977.

Batchelor, David. *Chromophobia.* London: Reaktion Books Ltd., 2000.

Birren, Faber. *Color & Human Response.* New York: Van Nostrand Reinhold Company, 1978.

———. *Color Psychology and Color Therapy.* Secaucus, N.J.: Citadel Books, 1961.

———. *Functional Color.* New York: The Crimson Press, 1937.

———. *The Story of Color.* Westport, Com.: The Crimson Press, 1941.

Chan, Tak Cheung, and Garth F. Petrie. "The Brain Learns Better in Well-Designed School Environments." *Classroom Leadership,* 2, no. 3 (1998).

"Color Symbolism." Color 4 Business, Carnright Design, www.carnrightdesign.com/color4business/color_symbolism.htm

"Emotional and Psychological Impact of Color." Color 4 Business, Carnright Design, www.carnrightdesign.com/color4business_impact.htm

Delamare, François, and Bernard Guineau. *Colors, the Story of Dyes and Pigments.* New York: Harry N. Abrams, 2000.

Finlay, Victoria. *Color: A Natural History of the Palette.* New York: Ballantine Books, 2002.

Gage, John. *Colour and Meaning: Art, Science, and Symbolism.* London: Thames and Hudson, 1999.

Gass, William. *On Being Blue: A Philosophical Inquiry.* Boston: David R. Godine, 1976.

Hass, Nancy. "Don't Use That Tone With Me." *New York Times Magazine,* Home Design issue, April 13, 2003.

Johnson, David. "Psychology of Color." Infoplease.com, www.infoplease.com/spot/colors1.html

"The Meaning of Colors." S.F. Heart, www.sfheart.com/color.html

The Oxford Dictionary of Quotations. 3rd ed. New York: Oxford University Press, 1980.

Paint Resource Library. The Rohm and Hass Paint Quality Institute, www.paintquality.com/library/index.html

Rubenzahl, Moe. "The Man's Guide to Color." Eyes of Men, www.eyesofmen.com/articles/humor/color.htm

Saunders, Gill. *Wallpaper in Interior Decoration.* New York: Watson-Guptill Publications, 2002.

Sutcliffe, John. *Paint: Decorating with Water-Based Paints.* New York: Henry Holt and Company, 1996.

Theroux, Alexander. *The Primary Colors.* New York: Henry Holt and Company, 1994.

Thompson, G. "Japanese Traditional and Ceremonial Colors." Temarikai.com, www.temarikai.com

Wallace, Robert. *The World of Van Gogh, 1853–1890.* New York: Time-Life Books, 1972.

"What Colors Mean." Fact Monster, www.factmonster.com/ipka/A0769383.html

Wittgenstein, Ludwig. *Remarks on Colour.* Berkeley: University of California Press, 1978.

Wood, Betty. *The Healing Power of Color.* Rochester, Vt.: Destiny Books, 1984.

index